T0053951

A KID'S GUIDE TO
THE CHINESE ZODIAC

A KID'S GUIDE TO THE CHINESE ZODIAC

Animal Horoscopes, Legendary Myths,
and Practical Uses for Ancient Wisdom

AARON HWANG

Illustrated by **QU LAN**

RP|KIDS
PHILADELPHIA

Running Press Kids
Hachette Book Group
1290 Avenue of the Americas, New York, NY 10104
www.runningpress.com/rpkids
@runningpresskids

Printed in China

First Edition: December 2023

Published by Running Press Kids, an imprint of Perseus Books, LLC,
a subsidiary of Hachette Book Group, Inc. The Running Press Kids name
and logo are trademarks of the Hachette Book Group.

The Hachette Speakers Bureau provides a wide range of authors for speaking events.
To find out more, go to www.hachettespeakersbureau.com
or email HachetteSpeakers@hbgusa.com.

Running Press books may be purchased in bulk for business, educational, or promotional
use. For more information, please contact your local bookseller or the Hachette Book
Group Special Markets Department at Special.Markets@hbgusa.com.

Print book cover and interior design by Frances J. Soo Ping Chow.

Library of Congress Cataloging-in-Publication Data has been applied for.
Library of Congress Control Number: 2022061094

ISBNs: 978-0-7624-8211-5 (hardcover), 978-0-7624-8212-2 (ebook)

1010

10 9 8 7 6 5 4 3 2 1

CONTENTS

INTRODUCTION

B EFORE THE INVENTION OF THE CALENDAR, IT WAS HARD TO keep track of time. Eventually even nature became confused. Winter snow blew in summer, autumn leaves fell in spring. The stars themselves wobbled out of synchronization.

It was amid this chaos that the Jade Emperor decided something must be done. So he summoned all his finest ministers, astrologers, and mathematicians, and after much argument and computation, they produced a solution:

A calendar would be made, mapping the flow of qì through the universe, plotting its repeating rhythms through the hours, days, months, and years, so that fate could be predicted and life could again proceed harmoniously. The Jade Emperor thus declared a race among animals. The first twelve to reach Heaven's gate would receive a permanent place of honor by having a phase in the calendar named after them. The winners arrived in this order: Rat, Ox, Tiger, Rabbit, Dragon, Snake, Horse, Goat, Monkey, Rooster, Dog, and Pig.

Each animal had a unique character, and together they helped us keep track not just of time but of the *nature* of time. With this calendar, people could tell not only if it was summer or winter, or day or night, they could also know if it was a time meant for growth, or work, or relaxation.

By just looking at the calendar, people, animals, ghosts, and stars could all know what destiny had in store for them and what cycles of energy had guided them since birth. This did not make the world a perfect place, but it at least made it a fraction more knowable.

This is just a story, one of many. But all good stories are built around a truth. The calendar invented in this story still exists today as the Chinese Zodiac and the Four Pillars of Destiny. Both are still used by people around the world to predict their destiny and discover new meaning about themselves.

WHAT IS THE CHINESE ZODIAC?

You may have already heard of the Chinese Zodiac or know the animal matched to your birth year. But there's so much more to this ancient practice. The Zodiac calendar is called the Four Pillars of Destiny because there are *four* cycles, not just one. There's one for Year, one for Month, one for Day, and one for Hour, each turning independently like four hands on a clock. That means every moment has not just one animal horoscope but four, as each pillar cycles through sixty possibilities, derived from twelve animal signs and five element signs. For over two thousand years these cycles have continued uninterrupted, slowly ticking through over twelve million unique combinations.

WHAT DOES THE
CHINESE ZODIAC TELL ME?

For thousands of years, people have turned to the Pillars to learn more about themselves, using it as a guide in decision-making for matters as small as what they should wear and as large as whom they should marry. The animals and elements that were present at your birth are the ones that say the most about who you might be! They record the energy that flowed through the universe in the moment that you entered it, and that energy guides you your entire life.

These different combinations manifest themselves in people's lives in different ways. For example, if you were born in late March at noon you are guided by both the sensitive Rabbit (your month) and the head-strong Horse (your hour). These guides might not seem compatible at first, but each can teach you something in different parts of your life. You might find the Rabbit's sharp-eared but anxious tendencies rule your teens, while the thundering Horse guides you in old age. Or perhaps around strangers you follow the Rabbit's sharp instincts, but among people you trust, your competitive and powerful Horse side takes the lead.

Some people find there is one animal that they relate to above the other three, one they most identify with. While this is exciting, it's good to keep in mind that you are fluid, complex, and capable of change; what resonates with you now might not resonate with you in the future, or might resonate differently. Following the impulses of any part of your Four Pillars can help you get in touch with aspects of yourself you haven't yet discovered. After all, nobody can be summed up by just one animal sign. No one is that simple. Who you really are is drawn from your unique combination of qualities, your unique life. This book can help you understand it.

Of course, nobody can tell you who to be, and there are a lot of ways to think about the cosmos. Think of this book and the Chinese Zodiac less as a rule and more as a tool to decipher the world around you. It can be a way to learn more about yourself and find harmony with the rest of the universe on the way.

THE ZODIAC CYCLE

⟵ ⟶

THE CHINESE ZODIAC COMES FROM THE IDEA THAT JUST AS the physical stuff of the universe (the stars, the tides, day and night) all move in patterns, so too does the energy that makes us who we are.

To symbolize the different forms this energy can take, the Zodiac's founders combined the cycle of twelve animals with the cycle of five elements to capture a total of sixty different types of energy. Just like the seasons, these animals and elements have a natural order, where one gives way to the other in an infinite cycle.

The animals proceed in this pattern: Rat → Ox → Tiger → Rabbit → Dragon → Snake → Horse → Goat → Monkey → Rooster → Dog → Pig → repeat.

The elements proceed in this pattern: Wood → Fire → Earth → Metal → Water → repeat, with the added wrinkle that each element occurs twice before moving to the next one.

This means when you track the Elements and Animals simultaneously to get the full cycle of sixty, it looks like the chart on the following page (reading each column from top to bottom).

Wood Rat	Fire Rat	Earth Rat	Metal Rat	Water Rat
Wood Ox	Fire Ox	Earth Ox	Metal Ox	Water Ox
Fire Tiger	Earth Tiger	Metal Tiger	Water Tiger	Wood Tiger
Fire Rabbit	Earth Rabbit	Metal Rabbit	Water Rabbit	Wood Rabbit
Earth Dragon	Metal Dragon	Water Dragon	Wood Dragon	Fire Dragon
Earth Snake	Metal Snake	Water Snake	Wood Snake	Fire Snake
Metal Horse	Water Horse	Wood Horse	Fire Horse	Earth Horse
Metal Goat	Water Goat	Wood Goat	Fire Goat	Earth Goat
Water Monkey	Wood Monkey	Fire Monkey	Earth Monkey	Metal Monkey
Water Rooster	Wood Rooster	Fire Rooster	Earth Rooster	Metal Rooster
Wood Dog	Fire Dog	Earth Dog	Metal Dog	Water Dog
Wood Pig	Fire Pig	Earth Pig	Metal Pig	Water Pig

After the Wood Rat comes the Wood Ox, and then the Fire Tiger, and so on. Continue this through all sixty signs to the Water Pig, and you get the complete Zodiac cycle!

YOUR COMPLETE BIRTH CHART: FOUR PILLARS AND EIGHT WORDS

At all times, the four Zodiac cycles for Year, Month, Day, and Hour are constantly in motion. Where these cycles were at the time of your birth is what is known as your Four Pillars. The animal and element that correlate to the year, month, day, and hour you were born results in a total of four animals and four elements. Together they make up your complete birth chart, also known as your Bāzi, or Eight Words.

HOUR	DAY	MONTH	YEAR
Hour Element	Day Element	Month Element	Year Element
Hour Animal	Day Animal	Month Animal	Year Animal

Unfortunately, most clocks don't reflect time according to the Chinese Zodiac! Unless you're keeping careful track, it's hard to know that, for example, October 1, 2022, falls on the Day of the Fire Pig.

The traditional method of calculating the signs is to look at a *Tung Shing* or Hsia Calendar. These are ancient calendars—the closest thing to a Zodiac clock that there is. You can buy physical versions of these calendars, or search for online versions.

The easiest way to learn the signs of a particular time is simply to Google "Bāzi calculator" to access websites that do the calculation for you, whether you're trying to find your full birth chart or the Four Pillars for a given moment. Some of these websites will go into more detail than this book covers, so if you're the type of person who needs to know your entire chart to feel satisfied, an online resource is your best bet for accuracy.

HOUR AND MONTH

Here are some simple charts for the Hour, Month, and Year pillars that are more or less always true with regard to when each animal sign is active within these cycles.

HOUR		MONTH	
11p.m.–1a.m.	Hour of the Rat	Dec. 7–Jan. 6	Month of the Rat
1a.m.–3a.m.	Hour of the Ox	Jan. 6–Feb. 4	Month of the Ox
3a.m.–5a.m.	Hour of the Tiger	Feb. 4–Mar. 6	Month of the Tiger
5a.m.–7a.m.	Hour of the Rabbit	Mar. 6–Apr. 5	Month of the Rabbit
7a.m.–9a.m.	Hour of the Dragon	Apr. 5–May 6	Month of the Dragon
9a.m.–11a.m.	Hour of the Snake	May 6–June 6	Month of the Snake
11a.m.–1p.m.	Hour of the Horse	June 6–July 7	Month of the Horse
1p.m.–3p.m.	Hour of the Goat	July 7–Aug. 8	Month of the Goat
3p.m.–5p.m.	Hour of the Monkey	Aug. 8–Sept. 8	Month of the Monkey
5p.m.–7p.m.	Hour of the Rooster	Sept. 8–Oct. 8	Month of the Rooster
7p.m.–9p.m.	Hour of the Dog	Oct. 8–Nov. 7	Month of the Dog
9p.m.–11p.m.	Hour of the Pig	Nov. 7–Dec. 7	Month of the Pig

So, for example, at four p.m. on November 25, the Monkey is the hour sign and the Pig is the month sign. One way to remember these charts is to memorize the order of the Zodiac animals. Then all you need to do is remember that the Rat rules midnight and most of December (both twelve a.m. and the twelfth month), and it isn't hard to count forward or backward from there.

YEAR

For the Year pillar, a good way to calculate the signs is to remember that 2020 was the year of the Metal Rat. From there, you can count forward or backward. (Again, it's helpful if you have the order of the animals memorized.) But, in case you hate counting, here's the full collection of our current sixty-year cycle and the one before.

ZODIAC CYCLE 1924–1983		
YEAR	ANIMAL	ELEMENT
1924	Rat	Wood
1925	Ox	Wood
1926	Tiger	Fire
1927	Rabbit	Fire
1928	Dragon	Earth
1929	Snake	Earth
1930	Horse	Metal
1931	Goat	Metal
1932	Monkey	Water
1933	Rooster	Water
1934	Dog	Wood
1935	Pig	Wood
1936	Rat	Fire

ZODIAC CYCLE 1984–2043		
YEAR	ANIMAL	ELEMENT
1984	Rat	Wood
1985	Ox	Wood
1986	Tiger	Fire
1987	Rabbit	Fire
1988	Dragon	Earth
1989	Snake	Earth
1990	Horse	Metal
1991	Goat	Metal
1992	Monkey	Water
1993	Rooster	Water
1994	Dog	Wood
1995	Pig	Wood
1996	Rat	Fire

1937	Ox	Fire
1938	Tiger	Earth
1939	Rabbit	Earth
1940	Dragon	Metal
1941	Snake	Metal
1942	Horse	Water
1943	Goat	Water
1944	Monkey	Wood
1945	Rooster	Wood
1946	Dog	Fire
1947	Pig	Fire
1948	Rat	Earth
1949	Ox	Earth
1950	Tiger	Metal
1951	Rabbit	Metal
1952	Dragon	Water
1953	Snake	Water
1954	Horse	Wood
1955	Goat	Wood
1956	Monkey	Fire
1957	Rooster	Fire
1958	Dog	Earth
1959	Pig	Earth
1960	Rat	Metal
1961	Ox	Metal
1962	Tiger	Water
1963	Rabbit	Water

1997	Ox	Fire
1998	Tiger	Earth
1999	Rabbit	Earth
2000	Dragon	Metal
2001	Snake	Metal
2002	Horse	Water
2003	Goat	Water
2004	Monkey	Wood
2005	Rooster	Wood
2006	Dog	Fire
2007	Pig	Fire
2008	Rat	Earth
2009	Ox	Earth
2010	Tiger	Metal
2011	Rabbit	Metal
2012	Dragon	Water
2013	Snake	Water
2014	Horse	Wood
2015	Goat	Wood
2016	Monkey	Fire
2017	Rooster	Fire
2018	Dog	Earth
2019	Pig	Earth
2020	Rat	Metal
2021	Ox	Metal
2022	Tiger	Water
2023	Rabbit	Water

1964	Dragon	Wood		2024	Dragon	Wood
1965	Snake	Wood		2025	Snake	Wood
1966	Horse	Fire		2026	Horse	Fire
1967	Goat	Fire		2027	Goat	Fire
1968	Monkey	Earth		2028	Monkey	Earth
1969	Rooster	Earth		2029	Rooster	Earth
1970	Dog	Metal		2030	Dog	Metal
1971	Pig	Metal		2031	Pig	Metal
1972	Rat	Water		2032	Rat	Water
1973	Ox	Water		2033	Ox	Water
1974	Tiger	Wood		2034	Tiger	Wood
1975	Rabbit	Wood		2035	Rabbit	Wood
1976	Dragon	Fire		2036	Dragon	Fire
1977	Snake	Fire		2037	Snake	Fire
1978	Horse	Earth		2038	Horse	Earth
1979	Goat	Earth		2039	Goat	Earth
1980	Monkey	Metal		2040	Monkey	Metal
1981	Rooster	Metal		2041	Rooster	Metal
1982	Dog	Water		2042	Dog	Water
1983	Pig	Water		2043	Pig	Water

Also note the Astrological New Year doesn't start until February 4. So if you're born in January or early February, you're still part of the previous Zodiac year!

For example: someone born at noon on January 12, 1983, is actually year of the Water Dog, since the Pig won't start until February 4. Checking the Month and Hour charts also shows this person's Month is Ox, and their Hour is Horse.

You might be wondering why there isn't a nifty chart for calculating signs for the Day pillar. That's because unlike the hours and months, which divide neatly into twelve, and the years, which move slowly enough to keep track of, the Gregorian calendar is 365 days long, a number that does not mesh at all with the Zodiac cycle of twelve. Throw in the complications of leap years, and it requires relatively complicated equations to convert a Gregorian date into a Zodiac Day sign. For similar reasons, there just isn't a straightforward way to calculate the elements for the Month, Day, and Hour pillars. If you want to learn your entire birth chart, including your Day signs or other elements, or if you have an edge case that falls between months (for example, January 6), then it may make sense to consult an official calendar or plug your birth details into an online Bāzi calculator.

For someone just getting started, learning even just a few of your signs can give you a lot to think about. What parts of you do the signs speak to? Which parts are still a mystery? Calculate Zodiac signs for your friends and family members, too, to see how well your stars align.

WHAT DO
THE SIGNS MEAN?

EACH ELEMENT AND ANIMAL STANDS FOR A CERtain way of approaching life. They indicate strengths and weaknesses, and ways to consider doing things. The next section will explore each of the animals and elements and give some general advice on how someone with a certain sign can tackle their problems, manage their relationships, and find their center.

THE ELEMENTS

THE FIVE ELEMENTS, ALSO CALLED THE "WŬXÍNG," DESCRIBE states of being that exist in a cycle and are endlessly in transition. Each element strengthens and creates the next, guaranteeing that the loop naturally continues. This section explores what each element represents and how each can be strengthened or balanced.

WOOD

Wood is the element of beginnings. It represents the blank slate, the open mind, the empty field in which something new can sprout. Paired with a Zodiac animal, Wood manifests a more flexible version of that animal, humble and ready for growth.

Wood is associated with childhood, art, and readiness. A clean room, a blank sheet of paper, a fresh morning are all things that carry Wood energy. When abundant, the Wood element makes us open-minded and prepared to learn. When overabundant, Wood can make us naive and indecisive.

TO STRENGTHEN: Water strengthens Wood. Taking deep breaths, letting go, meditating, and taking a nap are all good Water element activities that can feed the openness of Wood.

TO BALANCE: Wood is balanced by the cutting bite of Metal. Making pros and cons lists, doing research, and planning in advance are all Metal element activities that can protect the vulnerabilities of Wood.

FIRE

Fire is the element of inspiration, which takes root in the readiness of Wood. It represents creativity, emotions, and the burning passion that brings about change in the world. Pairing a Zodiac animal with Fire manifests a more passionate version of that animal, full of energy and volatility.

Fire is associated with intellect and young adulthood. Laughter, daydreaming, and strong emotions of all kinds are things that carry Fire energy. When abundant, the Fire element makes us decisive, energetic, and flashing with genius. Without balance, Fire can become moody and unstable.

TO STRENGTHEN: Wood strengthens Fire. Going for a walk, doing something without judgment, and letting yourself try something new are all good Wood element activities that can encourage the inspiration of Fire.

TO BALANCE: Fire is balanced by the dousing release of Water. Taking deep breaths, letting go, meditating, and taking a nap are all Water element activities that can curb the dangers of Fire.

EARTH

Earth is the element of reality, left in the aftermath of Fire. It represents stability, action, and the material world as it is, without names or labels. Having an animal paired with the Earth element manifests a more practical, enduring version of that animal, ready to build and protect a stable life.

Earth is associated with buildings, patience, balance, and adulthood. Doing work, creating something, and taking action are all activities with Earth energy. When abundant, the Earth element makes us resilient, practical, and industrious. Without balance, Earth can become stagnant, immobile, and depressed.

TO STRENGTHEN: Fire strengthens Earth. Letting yourself feel, laugh and cry, chase your dreams, and follow your intuition are all good Fire element activities that can inspire you to the action of Earth.

TO BALANCE: Earth is balanced by the tender roots of Wood. Trying something new, doing something without judgment, or going outside to break out of your usual orbit are all Wood element activities that can break up the stasis of Earth.

METAL

Metal is the element of concepts. If Earth is a physical object like a table, then Metal is the idea, the *concept* of a table. The Declaration of Independence is just ink on paper. The ink and the paper are physical, they're Earth. But the ideas the Declaration represents are Metal. Once we interact with things, with objects, we can't help but label them, define them, start having ideas about them. In this way, Earth leads to Metal.

An animal paired with the Metal element manifests a more meticulous, detailed, and rigid version of that animal, one that observes and breaks things down into keen ideas. Metal is associated with accuracy, control, and middle age. Poetry, mathematics, and money all have Metal energy, for they are systems that rely on concept and symbol as much as physical materials. When abundant, the Metal element makes us perceptive, rational, and disciplined. Without balance, Metal can become heavy-handed, inflexible, and blunt.

TO STRENGTHEN: Earth strengthens Metal. Doing work, getting physically involved with something, or showing up to an event are all good Earth element activities that can encourage new concepts and lessons for Metal.

TO BALANCE: Metal is softened by the forging heat of Fire. Follow your instincts without overthinking. Laugh, cry, let your emotions run their course. All these are Fire element activities that can soften the rough rigidity of metal.

WATER

Water is the element of letting go. Ask why long enough, and almost any idea will break down. In this way, Metal leads to Water. Water represents death, endings, letting go, and the unknown. Having an animal paired with Water manifests a more introspective version of that animal, flexible and ready to look beyond. Water is associated with spirituality, wisdom, old age, and emotions. But unlike Fire, which is about the emotions themselves, Water is about the unknown place inside us where emotions come from. Sleep, relaxation, and admitting you might not have the answer all have Water energy. When abundant, Water makes us wise and forgiving. Without balance, Water can become unhinged and despairing.

TO STRENGTHEN: Water builds in the rigid cracks and crevices of Metal. Breaking something down into its basic attributes, doing research, and asking questions like "why" are all Metal element activities that help capture the release of Water.

TO BALANCE: Water is absorbed by the presence of Earth. Doing work, getting physically involved with something, and attending events are all Earth element activities that can absorb Water and keep it from dissolving everything.

THE ANIMALS

PAIRED WITH THE FIVE ELEMENTS ARE THE TWELVE ANIMALS, also called the Twelve Earthly Branches.

Each of the Twelve Animals represents a way of being that becomes powerful at certain hours, months, days, and years. Remember, each person has four animal signs as well as four elements. This makes for an incredibly rich birth chart, one in which the reality of your life will always be more nuanced than any one sign can capture.

Each animal in this ancient practice provides insight on the strengths and challenges of certain ways of being. Particularly if the animal is part of our birth chart, it can teach us a lot about how we might behave, or how we might *choose* to behave in order to achieve our intended outcomes. This section will delve into the characteristics of each animal and its mythic roles, and offer advice on how to make the most of each animal's unique approach to life.

THE RAT

YEAR: 1960, 1972, 1984, 1996, 2008, 2020, 2032
MONTH: December 7–January 6
HOUR: 11:00 p.m.–1:00 a.m.

Ambitious and clever, the Rat rises in the midnight hours of eleven p.m. to one a.m., when a new day is born, and during the heart of Winter when the nights are long. If you were born during either, the Rat is one of your signs! Unorthodox, flexible, and persistent, Rat signs can solve any problem, finding the smallest gaps in the greatest walls and working their way through.

FAMILY

Rats are nest builders. They feel most secure when they've built up a happy, well-protected home, and this includes a group of loved ones that feels secure. The Rat sign knows that there's strength in numbers. When things get rough, what's more reassuring than someone you can rely on?

HOW TO EXPRESS LOVE: Rats have an eye for detail, an eye for the little things. Turn this watchful gaze on the people you care about to better understand them, in case one day they seek out your help. Reach out when you think they're feeling down and be there for them when they're ready to celebrate. They'll appreciate having someone so thoughtful around.

HOW TO BE HEARD: Often Rat signs prefer to take the path of least resistance. They see it as plain common sense, but sometimes doing the hard thing can be necessary. Staying silent may feel easier in the short term but can become just another kind of trap in the long term. Don't let yourself get trapped! Rat signs have good instincts. If you have something you want to speak up about, others would be wise to listen.

FRIENDSHIP

Rats are survivors, always capable of holding their own, but they're at their strongest in a group. Rat signs make natural leaders, subtle and effective. They get along well with the Ox, Dragon, and Monkey.

BEING SUPPORTIVE: Small but mighty, Rats are champions of underdogs everywhere. You stand up for your friends against the world's injustice, even when keeping your head down might be easier. People admire your bravery and the clever ways you get around even the biggest obstacles.

Rats have a keen sense of organization, even if they're the only ones who understand it. They recognize that tiny details are what make the world go round. When your friends are scattered and confused, you have the skills to make a plan of action and lead them to success.

WORKING THROUGH PROBLEMS: Rats are so good at spotting and solving problems that sometimes they jump to conclusions too quickly. A Rat sign is the first to notice if something isn't working out, and also the first to cut the problem loose. Don't be too quick to give up! Talk to the people around you and see if they share your doubts. If they do, you'll be able to work through the issue together, and if they don't, you can learn their point of view. You might find out there's less to worry about than you feared.

SCHOOL

STRENGTHS: Natural problem solvers, Rats have all the skills they need to excel in school. You are good at poking and prodding and handling things with precision. Even very complicated subjects make sense to you once you cut them down to size.

You excel when you face your problems with practicality, piece by piece, like a mouse storing grain for the winter. Break your to-do list into a series of small, manageable tasks, and finish them off one by one. Rat signs know mountains are conquered one inch at a time, and that is where they are strongest.

CHALLENGES: The Rat is an unconventional thinker, but this goes hand in hand with overthinking. You may be quick to spot problems and shy away as a result. If a Rat thinks a game is rigged, they will not want to play. Be wary of letting skepticism and fear keep you from action. Risk-taking is a part of life, and sometimes the biggest risk, one that can be fatal, is not playing at all. You can be good at anything if you just give yourself a chance.

ACTIVITIES WITH RAT SIGN ENERGY

- ◆ Architecture
- ◆ Jobs and business (mowing lawns, babysitting, fundraisers, etc.)
- ◆ Robotics
- ◆ Sketching

Rats excel in many fields, from art to business to the sciences. Anything where they can bring together a satisfying project with hard work, sharp attention, and a unique approach suits the Rat just fine.

FINDING YOUR CENTER

When you see as clearly as the Rat, it's easy to notice that the world is big and you are small. Many Rats wrestle with fear of the chaos and threats they notice all around them. Surrounding yourself with plans of action and people you trust can help you feel more prepared.

When you do feel stress pushing you into a panic, try to unplug from your worries and take a deep breath. You may be small but you're not alone. Talk to someone you trust and see if they can help keep you from thinking in circles. Burrow to the heart of the issue. Fear isn't something to be ashamed of—it's something to be understood.

THE RAT WHO WOULD MARRY THE SUN

Once upon a time, a family of rats wanted to arrange a marriage for their beautiful daughter. They decided their daughter deserved the best and should only wed the most powerful being in the world: the Sun. But when the Sun heard their marriage proposal, his bright face dimmed in shame. "I am not the most powerful," the Sun admitted. "For the vast Cloud can smother even my strongest rays!"

Impressed, the rats sought out the Cloud, to see if he would marry their daughter. But when they found him, the Cloud also admitted he was only second best. "The roaring Wind blows me whichever way he pleases!" But the Wind, too, knew a superior: the Wall, who shrugged off even the fiercest gales.

The rats journeyed to the Wall and proposed, but the Wall laughed, shaking down to his bricks and mortar. "There's someone much mightier than me," said the Wall, "who chews through my deepest foundations every single day."

The Wall then directed the family to a hole at his base where a handsome young rat lived.

Versions of this story are told around the world. They all capture an idea that is very near and dear to the Rat: power is often just a matter of perspective—in the right situation, even the tiniest person can be mighty.

HOW TO SECURE
GOOD LUCK

The Rat's usual lucky colors are gold, blue, and green. This doesn't mean you have to change your style, but keep an eye out for those colors. If you see them, the universe may be trying to tell you something. A small token or accessory in those colors may bring you luck as well, and help you feel like you have a secret you can rely on in your back pocket.

The Rat's lucky numbers are 2, 3, 6, and 8, and any numbers that combine those digits. Their lucky flowers are the African violet and any type of lily.

THE YEAR OF THE RAT

After the Pig settles down and wipes the slate clean, the Rat is prepared for a new beginning. The beginning of the twelve-year Zodiac cycle, Rat years are a time for dreaming, planning, and beginning. This applies to everyone, not just those with Rat in their birth chart. When the year of the Rat rolls around, harness the Rat's practicality and look forward, making the changes and preparations that will be necessary to thrive in the upcoming years. Like a mouse building a nest one scrap at a time, your small steps lay the groundwork for future success.

Rat years also emphasize community. Small individuals who band together create a mighty force. People are a resource just as important as money or shelter or success. Make sure you have people you can count on, and you'll make short work of this year's troubles.

THE OX

YEAR: 1961, 1973, 1985, 1997, 2009, 2021, 2033
MONTH: January 6–February 4
HOUR: 1:00 a.m.–3:00 a.m.

Persistent and tireless, the Ox stands for the early hours of one to three a.m. and the end of Winter. If you were born during either, you have the Ox as a sign! Reliable and strong, you have a particular way you like to get things done. You push forward at your own pace and can pull the heaviest loads or break the toughest ground.

FAMILY

When the people you love need someone they can count on, they look to you. You have thick skin and can weather a lot, but this same toughness can also make it hard for you to understand the sensitivity of others.

HOW TO EXPRESS LOVE: The Ox often assumes the best way to show care is through diligence. You are not one for big displays of affection, preferring instead to reliably show up day after day and not cause drama. Simple gestures done regularly are a great way for an Ox to show appreciation. Ask the other person how their day was or help them with a simple task in the morning, and your strength will make everyone's load lighter.

HOW TO BE HEARD: Thick-skinned and durable, most Oxen can suffer in silence for a long time before they complain or are even aware that anything is wrong. Being slow to speak can be okay if you use that time to think over what you want to say. You can say more in one sentence than others might say in a whole day if you take the time to say it right.

Try to pay attention to your own feelings. Many Oxen are slow to anger or even discomfort, but once upset they are equally difficult to soothe. A raging bull is a dangerous force, and if you start feeling the need to throw your weight around just to make your point, things may end up broken.

FRIENDSHIP

The sign of the Ox is a powerful ally. Constant, unbreakable, and unafraid of hardship, they combine reliability with a gentle strength. Ox signs get along harmoniously with the Rat, Snake, and Rooster.

BEING SUPPORTIVE: Ox signs enjoy helping others. You are a pillar of your friend group, and you protect the people you're close to. Sometimes you might even take too much responsibility, putting the weight of the world on your back and assuming every problem you can't prevent is your fault.

Together with your naturally sedate and reserved personality, this might make it hard to get close to people. Just remember you aren't alone. Don't be afraid to open up and let other people help you. This lets people know they have your trust.

WORKING THROUGH PROBLEMS: Some Ox signs struggle with being aloof. They are so sturdy that they might not notice other people's discomfort. Like a bull in a china shop, even a very careful Ox may occasionally break something or cause offense. Good communication can help prevent this; when in doubt, tell your friends it's okay to be up-front with you. The more their concerns are laid out plain and simple, the better you will be able to navigate them without concern.

Remember that strength is a responsibility as much as a virtue. Just because you may have a thick skin, it doesn't mean that everyone around you will be the same. Try to keep an open mind and be accepting of other points of view.

SCHOOL

STRENGTHS: Diligent, hardworking, and unafraid of routine, Ox signs make good students. You can slog through the most difficult assignments and push through the daily annoyances that leave other people bogged down and distraught, without complaint. In group assignments nobody pulls their weight like you, although deep down you are more concerned with seeing things done *right* than with who is actually in charge.

To capitalize on your strengths, set yourself up for success. Routines work well for Oxen, so set one up that nourishes you and sees you living the life you want to live.

CHALLENGES: Oxen plow the same rows day after day, and while this makes them diligent workers, it can also make them set in their ways. It's not easy to make an Ox change their course, and this can make you inflexible and traditional. You are slower to respond to change than others and may prefer well-practiced subjects to new ones.

Try to remember that all old fields were once new. The only antidote to the unfamiliar is practice. With a little patience and hard work, the unfamiliar will become familiar again, as long as you don't shy away from it.

ACTIVITIES WITH OX SIGN ENERGY

- Endurance sports (like cross-country running)
- Memory games
- Musical instruments
- Knitting/crochet

Any activity that requires extended focus, repetition, and a mind excited by hard work is a good fit for the enduring Ox.

FINDING YOUR CENTER

The Ox sign's energy is one of chill. While the Rat may scurry to and fro, anxious about a hundred problems and dangers, the Ox is calm and sedate. Oxen know there is not much out there that can harm them, and this gives them a natural, slow-moving security.

Picking a simple task that calms you down and lets you feel productive, like knitting or sketching, can be a good way to unwind. On the other hand, after a long day of work it can also be rejuvenating to seek out something or someone that excites you or makes you laugh. This can help you break new ground, take a load off, and just have fun.

OXEN IN CHINESE MYTH

For helping humans plow the fields, and thus forever changing the shape of society, the Ox holds many roles in Chinese myth.

Niutou, or "Oxhead," was created when the King of the Underworld took pity on the soul of a diligent Ox. As a reward for working hard every single day of his life, the ox's soul was transformed into Oxhead, a messenger of the Underworld with the head of an ox and the body of a man. Along with his partner Horseface, hardworking Oxhead escorts dead souls to the Underworld, where they wait to receive judgment.

Another legendary beast associated with the Ox is the Kui. This strange creature appears as a bright blue ox with no horns and just one foot. But that one foot is all Kui needs—a god of storms, Kui stomps once on the Earth to create a crash of thunder and once in the water to make wind and rain. The name Kui means "awestruck," and it's been said that the Kui's hide can be used to make a godly drum whose fearful boom carries 500 leagues.

HOW TO SECURE GOOD LUCK

The Ox's lucky colors are typically green, yellow, and white. You don't need to change your life for these colors, but keep an eye out for them. Something important in those colors may bring you good luck and strengthen the Ox's naturally persevering spirit.

The Ox's lucky numbers are 1 and 4, and any combination of those digits. Your lucky flowers are the tulip and peach blossom.

THE YEAR OF THE OX

After the cunning Rat makes plans, the mighty Ox goes to work, laying the foundations for things to come. Ox years are years of perseverance, responsibility, and stability, a time for building and putting things in order. This applies to everyone, not just those with the Ox in their birth chart. Move your favorite projects forward and get the work that needs to be done *done*. If anything in your life is starting to come apart, be it a friendship, a subject you're struggling with, or the tidiness of your room, Ox years are a perfect time to set them right.

On the other hand, during Ox years the Ox's stubbornness may come out. People may become stuck in their opinions and refuse to compromise. Avoid this by having a healthy humility. True wisdom comes from knowing how little you know and how much of a mystery the world remains, and from approaching the people around you with an open mind, ready to learn.

This is a year for planting. The crop may not come in right away, but when it does, you will be all the better for having gotten the work in now.

THE TIGER

- - - - - - - -

YEAR: 1962, 1974, 1986, 1998, 2010, 2022, 2034
MONTH: February 4–March 6
HOUR: 3:00 a.m.–5:00 a.m.

Striving and rebellious, the Tiger springs to life from three to five a.m. and welcomes both the Spring and the Lunar New Year. If you were born during either of these times, the Tiger is one of your signs! Competitive, creative, and fearless, you challenge yourself and the rules around you. You believe things can be new and better.

FAMILY

If you've ever owned a house cat, you know that they don't love to be controlled—and can't be. Tigers are independent souls and want a lot of territory—a caged Tiger is no one's friend. But when a Tiger is shown support and allowed to roam, no one's love is fiercer than theirs.

HOW TO EXPRESS LOVE: Courageous and passionate, the Tiger can bring energy to everyone around them. If you feel up to it, invite your loved ones along on one of your adventures. Whether that's playing a competitive game, exploring someplace new, or just lazing around in the sun, the Tiger knows how to enjoy life. Sharing an experience with someone else will add new layers to it and bring you closer together.

HOW TO BE HEARD: Natural rebels, most Tigers have no problem making themselves known. You don't shy away from conflict, and you regard rules and traditions with skepticism. You are passionate about your own ideas and always ready to fight to defend them.

While you are a natural fighter, don't overlook the power of empathy. Look for the big picture. Understanding another's point of view, and making them feel they are validated and heard, can have a persuasive power no amount of force can match. There's a time for claws and a time for treading softly.

FRIENDSHIP

People are drawn to the Tiger's courage and strength. You tend to mesh well with the high energy of the Horse and Dog, while the Pig and Rabbit are a relaxing comfort.

BEING SUPPORTIVE: Like all cats, Tigers can go from perfectly still to a blur in a single pounce. Not every friend will work at the same pace as you, and that's okay. Some of your friends will enjoy your hectic high-energy adventures, and some will enjoy being there to laze around with you on a day off. The more friends you make and the more things you try, the more options you'll have and the more you'll figure out what works for each relationship.

WORKING THROUGH PROBLEMS: Tigers are ferocious beasts, and sometimes this leads to conflict. If a situation makes you angry, try stepping away before things escalate. Find some distance—maybe go for a walk or read a book. Once you feel a little more like the emotions are behind you, interrogate them. Where did the feelings come from? Do you still feel them as strongly? Often your feelings tell you more about yourself than the other person.

Once you feel you understand yourself better, try considering the other person's point of view. How might they feel? Where might their feelings come from? This work will prepare you to express yourself with kindness instead of escalating the situation or backing away.

SCHOOL

STRENGTHS: Creative, competitive, and confident, Tiger signs are drawn to success. You know you can excel, and often this pushes you to do so. You set a high bar for yourself even if nobody else will.

To capitalize on your strengths, chase your ambitions. What is the fire that makes your dreams important to you? How can you honor those values in your day-to-day? Keeping your desire for excellence in mind will propel you to greater heights.

CHALLENGES: You are a natural fighter, so the rules, regulations, and deadlines of school may rub you the wrong way. You see no reason to do things you think are foolish or take orders from those you don't feel have earned your respect, and sometimes this might get you into trouble.

A healthy sense of skepticism can be a great asset if you also practice humility. True wisdom is knowing you have a lot left to learn. This openness is why beginners learn faster than experts. Try to remember that there is something of interest in every teacher, every peer, and every subject, if you can keep an open mind to look for it.

ACTIVITIES WITH
TIGER SIGN ENERGY

◆ Activism

◆ Fashion design

◆ Camping

◆ Solo sports (like running or boxing)

Tigers enjoy anything with a competitive edge where they can push themselves to be better than the day before. They also excel at anything that involves freedom, intuition, and quick thinking.

FINDING YOUR CENTER

Tigers thrive on new experiences and personal growth. While finding your center might involve doing something that makes you feel confident, like playing a game you love or hiking a familiar trail, it could also mean trying something new: a new sport, a new recipe, a new place to explore, a new person. Novelty is the heart of adventure.

Just remember, not everything is a battle to be won. While exploring, don't judge yourself too harshly. Tigers are often ready to fight, even with themselves. Treat yourself with compassion, and you'll find the world becomes a more peaceful place.

TIGERS IN CHINESE MYTH

As the most fearsome predator of Asia, the tiger has long captured the human imagination. A symbol of ferocity, power, and rulership, the tiger's stripes are said to mark it as royalty, with the Chinese word for king, "王" stamped in the marks on its forehead.

The most famous tiger of Chinese myth is the White Tiger. Along with the Phoenix, Tortoise, and Dragon, the White Tiger is one of the Four Sacred Beasts who guard the four directions. The White Tiger's direction is the west, where he serves as one of the largest constellations in Chinese astronomy.

Another mythic tiger is the Kaimingshou, also known as the Beast Facing East. With the body of a tiger and nine human faces, the Beast Facing East is guardian of the mythic Kunlun Mountain, which holds up the sky and serves as the home of countless gods, immortals, and legendary creatures. Just like the White Tiger, the Beast Facing East uses its ferocity to be a fearsome protector.

LUCKY TIGER

Considered inherently lucky, the Tiger's luckiest colors are blue, gray, and orange. Keeping these colors close can help bring out the Tiger's natural courage. Your lucky numbers are 1, 3, and 4. Keep an open mind; if you notice combinations of these digits and colors, the universe may be trying to tell you something. Make like a Tiger—when you see what you want, pounce on it!

The Tiger's lucky flowers are the yellow lily and cineraria.

THE YEAR OF THE TIGER

Like the storm that follows the calm, the rebellious Tiger follows the Ox. While the Ox is content to follow rules, the Tiger stirs things up, keeps things exciting. Tiger years can be full of explosive action or surprisingly quiet—this makes them hard to predict, much like the wild Tiger itself. That said, here is some Tiger year advice that can apply to everyone, not just those with Tiger in their birth chart.

Whereas the Ox year is full of preparation, the Tiger year lunges forward. Tiger years are a good time for change, for impulse and bravery, for chasing your dreams as a Tiger chases down prey. This doesn't mean every risk you take will pay off, but the Tiger knows there is more to be gained by taking chances than by doing nothing.

Tiger years can be just as dangerous as their predatory patron. Chaos and drama flourish in Tiger years. Try to remember that difficult times give us the opportunity to push ourselves and learn just how powerful we can be. The Tiger appreciates a challenge, and you too can wrestle with the beast.

THE RABBIT

YEAR: 1963, 1975, 1987, 1999, 2011, 2023, 2035
MONTH: March 6–April 5
HOUR: 5:00 a.m.–7:00 a.m.

Perceptive and sensitive, the Rabbit rises with the morning from five to seven a.m. and the blossom of Spring. If you were born during either of these times, the Rabbit is one of your signs! Attentive, intuitive, and delicate, you notice things nobody else would. You are full of potential, like a green shoot of grass rising come Spring.

FAMILY

Rabbits are unhappy when left alone, which is why pet owners often get them in pairs. Rabbits are used to living in big groups, building cozy nests and warrens together. Perhaps more than any other sign, you benefit from a safe environment where you can access the fullness of your vast potential.

HOW TO EXPRESS LOVE: As a Rabbit sign, you know that a comfy home is an important first step to happiness, and this can be a powerful expression of your care. You have a good eye for objects that bring people joy, and a good sense of home decor. You draw others to you when you make your home—or even just your room—more beautiful or clean, or get someone a special gift.

HOW TO BE HEARD: Rabbits are sensitive, slow to speak but always listening. It is easy to be timid when you have such keen ears. Every footstep sounds like it could be danger!

But for all their timidity, the Rabbit is full of potential, ready to blossom, containing the latent energy that will be brought forth in full force by the Dragon, the next sign in the Zodiac cycle.

If you have something difficult to say, try practicing it first with someone you feel safe with. They can help walk you through possible outcomes and help you feel more comfortable with speaking up.

FRIENDSHIP

Rabbits enjoy the safety and comfort of a group. They like getting close to people, especially those they can let their walls down around. They are natural friends with the Dog, Goat, Pig, and Tiger.

BEING SUPPORTIVE: With radar-like senses and a cautious manner, Rabbits rarely step on people's toes. If you feel fondly about the people around you, it is okay to let that show. People are often more drawn to kindness then coldness, and you have a natural sensitivity that draws people in. Letting your inner warmth show will let people know you care.

WORKING THROUGH PROBLEMS: When they sense danger in the wild, rabbits either run for the hills or hold perfectly still, hoping the problem will blow over and pass them by.

Many Rabbit signs are the same in their friendships—conflict averse to the end. When there's a problem, you might try to run away from the relationship rather than fix it, or you might hold still, ignoring the problem and hoping it goes away on its own.

Conflict is not inherently bad—no two people agree on everything, and the ability to address issues is an important skill in any relationship. If you allow yourself to do this from a place of concern for your friend's well-being as well as your own, you are doing everyone a favor.

SCHOOL

STRENGTHS: Rabbits are excellent listeners, capable of picking up on details that others overlook. To Rabbits, the whole world is a symphony of color and sound, and this makes it easier for them to find excitement in topics others might find dull.

CHALLENGES: The Rabbit sign's superb senses and natural timidity make it easy for them to get overwhelmed. In the classroom you may start to pick up on things besides the intended lesson: noises, movement, people around you, the general energy of the day. You may zone out or lose control of your focus. This is not a problem to be solved through force. If your mind wanders, instead of clamping down, try to channel it. Doodle while you take your notes. Write your wandering thoughts in the margins. Write a funny rhyme about today's lesson. Instead of stifling your creativity, guide it into what you are already doing, and you may create something fresh and unique.

ACTIVITIES WITH RABBIT SIGN ENERGY

◆ Writing

◆ Gardening

◆ Listening (to music, audiobooks, or podcasts)

◆ Working with animals

Rabbits excel at anything creative and have a keen eye for art that is hard to match. They also have a natural tenderness that makes them excellent nurturers, handling delicate things with care.

FINDING YOUR CENTER

For someone as sensitive as the Rabbit, it is most important to know how to find calm. Whenever you go anywhere, you are picking up on a hundred colors, energies, and noises, but most of them are just that—noise. Without a proper filter, the world can be overwhelming.

When you have time alone, find somewhere quiet to sit. Close your eyes, and just focus on your senses. Can you feel the clothes on your body, the breath on your lips? Every part of your body has its own set of nerves—how fine a sensation can you detect? For so much of life we take our senses for granted and block out so much of what we actually feel. This exercise can both calm your mind and help you better understand and control the ways your body makes sense of the world.

RABBITS IN CHINESE MYTH

Sensitive and secretive, the Rabbit in Chinese myth has long been associated with the moon. It used to be said they could reproduce by simply basking in moonlight, part of their incredible power to create life.

The most famous rabbit of Chinese myth is the Jade Rabbit, or the Rabbit in the Moon. In the story of his ascension, the Jade Rabbit wants to save a starving old man. However, while the monkey, otter, and jackal know how to find fruit, fish, and other scavenged food, Jade Rabbit knows only how to find grass, which cannot feed a man. So Jade Rabbit throws himself in the fire, offering his own body as food. But the fire doesn't burn the Jade Rabbit, at which point the starving old man reveals himself as the ruler of Heaven in disguise. Impressed by Jade Rabbit's generosity, the ruler grants him immortality and a place on the moon.

There the Jade Rabbit is said to work with a mortar and pestle, crafting the elixir of life sought after by mortals and deities alike.

HOW TO SECURE GOOD LUCK

The Rabbit's lucky colors are pink, red, purple, and blue. If you're a Rabbit sign, you may find these colors speak to you or provide comfort. You have a good eye for material things, so a physical token in your preferred color can give you something to focus on if you ever feel overwhelmed. Your lucky numbers are 3, 4, and 6, and any combination of these numbers.

The Rabbit's lucky flowers are the snapdragon, plantain lily, and jasmine.

THE YEAR OF THE RABBIT

They say March comes in like a lion and goes out like a lamb, but in the Chinese Zodiac, March comes in a Tiger and leaves a Rabbit. After the Tiger's stormy revolution, the world is made fresh and tender. There is room for new growth. The energy is tentative, fragile, and timid, and this is when the Rabbit peeks its head out.

Rabbit years are gentle but delicate. This applies to everyone, not just those with Rabbit in their birth chart. The previous years have come with change, and if you can look and listen like the Rabbit, you will discover new doors opened and opportunities sprouting up all around you. Rabbit years are listening years. If you try, you may notice new things about the people around you, the world, and yourself.

Remember—Rabbit years are sensitive, and that increased sensitivity can make the universe seem loud and overwhelming. So treat yourself with kindness and give yourself a chance to make the most of it.

THE DRAGON

YEAR: 1964, 1976, 1988, 2000, 2012, 2024, 2036
MONTH: April 5–May 6
HOUR: 7:00 a.m.–9:00 a.m.

The Dragon ascends to power in the close of Spring and the hours of seven to nine a.m., as the world floods with energy and vigor. If you were born during either of these times, the Dragon is one of your signs. Confident, imaginative, and multitalented, it seems like no limit can contain you.

FAMILY

Dragons are creatures of fantasy and limitless power. They scoff at gravity and chafe under rules. You are an incredible dynamo in your family, passionate and creative, but may have a hard time honoring the boundaries your loved ones have set.

HOW TO EXPRESS LOVE: A leader and innovator, you are capable of embarking on projects others would fold under. Grand and dramatic gestures may work well for you, like throwing someone a surprise party just to make them party. Go forth as your bold self! Just don't let visions of perfection stand in the way of imperfect joy.

HOW TO BE HEARD: The Dragon is in many ways the opposite of the Rabbit: where the Rabbit is timid and receptive to the world around them, the Dragon is capable of being a thundering monsoon, a force on the world that's impossible to ignore. Dragons often have no problem speaking their minds, but may have trouble accepting it when those around them don't agree.

Not all battles can be won, not even for the Dragon. Accepting this can be one of the Dragon's greatest challenges. Sometimes it is wiser to compromise or give than to expend your every resource trying to make the opposition bend or break.

FRIENDSHIP

Dragons are natural leaders—your confidence and big ideas suck people in like a tornado. The Rat, Monkey, Rooster, and Snake are natural companions to the Dragon.

BEING SUPPORTIVE: With your natural strength and generosity, you genuinely enjoy supporting the people around you. People are motivated by your energy, and you excel at rallying your friends to a cause or adventure that leaves everyone smiling.

Watch out for your more sensitive friends, the ones who are shy and have trouble advocating for themselves. Make sure you prioritize their feelings as well. The Dragon moves so fast and flies so high, it can be easy to leave people behind.

WORKING THROUGH PROBLEMS: When a Dragon fights, they rarely do so by half measures. You are used to being right and may struggle to empathize with, or even understand, those who don't agree. Don't underestimate the power of validating someone else. You may find that showing openness to someone else's ideas will make them more open to you in return.

SCHOOL

STRENGTHS: Dragons are high achievers. They like to have big plans of one kind or another, and they like to excel at what they do. Fantasy and innovation inspire you, and you enjoy projects and lessons that allow you to adventure outside the box.

To play to these strengths, try to work creativity into your lessons and assignments wherever you can. Even if others don't appreciate your style, what's important in the long run is that *you* feel more engaged with the work.

CHALLENGES: Most Dragons resent being told what to do. You prefer to achieve things in your own way, and the daily routine and schedules of school may leave you feeling stifled. If this is true, you might want to reframe school as an opportunity to challenge yourself. Make a list of things at school that you look forward to. Can you expand the list? Having even one thing to get excited about can make it easier to show up each day.

ACTIVITIES WITH DRAGON SIGN ENERGY

- ◆ Writing
- ◆ Reading
- ◆ Travel
- ◆ Journalism

The Dragon can do anything! It is said that the Chinese Dragon is made from the strengths of all the other Zodiac animals put together: Rat's whiskers, Ox's horns, Tiger's claws, Rabbit's eyes, Snake's body, Horse's legs, Goat's beard, Monkey's wit, Rooster's crest, Dog's ears, and Pig's snout. This is another way of saying a Dragon can be anything or succeed in any field, so long as it inspires them.

FINDING YOUR CENTER

As a Dragon sign, you have your head in the clouds, and this can make it difficult to keep your feet on the ground. Your whims and day-dreams can blow you around, making it hard to settle in any one place. Sometimes your plans and imaginings may even feel bigger than the real world.

Dreaming big is great, but staying grounded can help you recognize the beauty that is already around you. Try to take at least one moment each day to clear your mind and just observe your surroundings. Can you feel the air on your skin, the ground under your feet? What can you hear? What can you see?

You can also learn a lot by asking someone else for their perspective. None of us can see the whole world alone, but with more perspectives, our view can slowly become more complete.

DRAGONS IN CHINESE MYTH

Dragons are an important symbol in Chinese myth. Unlike Western Dragons, which are often winged, fire-breathing beasts, the Chinese Dragon is an intelligent and spiritual creature often associated with water—rivers and seas, rain and storms. These Dragons stride the sky as easily as the Earth and thus have no need for wings.

Some of the most famous dragons are the Four Dragon Kings, who preside over the four great bodies of water that are thought to mark the borders of ancient China. They are the Azure Dragon in the east, the Vermilion Dragon in the south, the White Dragon in the west, and the Black Dragon in the north. Most powerful of all is the fifth dragon—the Yellow Dragon of the center. The Yellow Dragon doesn't represent a body of water, but rather the Emperor, the Earth, and the rulership of China itself.

HOW TO SECURE GOOD LUCK

Gold, silver, and white are lucky colors for the Dragon, bringing out your natural power and majesty. That said, Dragons can pull off anything as long as it makes them feel confident. The Dragon's lucky numbers are 1, 6, and 7, and any combination of them might suggest an important signal or opportunity.

The clerodendrum, or bleeding heart, is your lucky flower, along with other draconic flora like the hyacinth, larkspur, and dragonhead.

THE YEAR OF THE DRAGON

In China, birth rates are known to go up in Dragon years because people are so eager to have children born under this lucky sign. The Dragon is known for prosperity and is said by some to drip gold, jade, and other precious things from its body like sweat.

In this sense Dragon years are times of fruition. This applies to everyone, not just people with Dragon in their birth chart. The hard work of the Rat and Ox, the revolution of the Tiger, the tender growth of the Rabbit, all come into their fullness in a Dragon year. Everything roars forward with endless possibility. Projects and people thrive, but problems may also be more explosive as things come to a breaking point. Pride might become a problem in the year of the Dragon, as people refuse to accept failure, take advice, or change course.

Try to remember, thriving doesn't mean never falling. Thriving means always rising again.

THE SNAKE

YEAR: 1965, 1977, 1989, 2001, 2013, 2025, 2037
MONTH: May 6–June 6
HOUR: 9:00 a.m.–11:00 a.m.

Full of mysterious power over life and death, the Snake ushers in the hours of nine to eleven a.m. and the early Summer, full of basking, life-giving heat. If you were born during either of these times, the Snake is one of your signs! Flexible, secretive, charming, and piercing, you wield the unknown and the subtle strength of giving way.

FAMILY

The Snake sign is naturally secretive and adaptable. With fluid forms and shedding skin, Snakes understand that identity can be malleable, meaning they can change. You are good at playing many roles, shifting yourself depending on who's around you.

HOW TO EXPRESS LOVE: With an array of keen and mysterious senses, the Snake has a knack for seeing the unseen. Listen to the people around you. Don't be afraid to ask them questions. You might be surprised by how much more you can learn about the people you think you know well already. This knowledge of others might also inspire you, giving you ideas for new ways to brighten their lives based on the careful attention you paid.

HOW TO BE HEARD: Snakes are notoriously private, and their true feelings may be mysterious even to themselves. Before you express yourself, take a moment to ask what it is you really want and why. Don't be afraid to be utterly honest—there's very little to gain from lying to yourself. Knowing your own mind will give you a more solid foundation from which to express yourself to others.

Furthermore, letting down your walls and letting people see your inner truth is a good way to let them know you respect them. Your loved ones know how much you value your privacy, and so your openness demonstrates real trust.

FRIENDSHIP

Snakes are natural charmers. You can adapt to the people around you with hypnotic ease, but you only want to truly befriend those you trust. The Ox, Rooster, Monkey, and Dragon mesh well with you.

BEING SUPPORTIVE: You take your friendships very seriously, prioritizing a few deep relationships over many casual ones. You are good at solving your friends' problems, sometimes predicting their troubles before even they are aware of them.

You can do your friends a lot of good by simply being available to listen. Let them talk through their problems, and you will find it natural to guide them to discover how they really feel. Nobody is easier to talk to than someone who is both receptive and tranquil, and your natural intuition makes you excellent at drawing out what lies within.

WORKING THROUGH PROBLEMS: Snakes adapt well to strife and change. They shed skins easily, and this also helps them move on. However, you keep your feelings to yourself, which may make it hard for your friends to know when you're hurting. You can't expect people to read your mind. If you want people to address your needs, you have to get comfortable with expressing them.

If you still can't see eye to eye, even once you understand each other, then it may be time to put your adaptability to work. Decide if this issue is more important than your friendship. You're great at moving on—but would you rather move on from this friend, or this fight?

SCHOOL

STRENGTHS: Snakes are intelligent and intuitive, cutting quickly to the heart of the matter. You are also good at reading people and can quickly work out what exactly is expected of you. Mastery gives you comfort, so you work hard at the fields that interest you. When it comes to speaking up, you're at your best when you hold your tongue until you are sure you have valuable insight to contribute. That's when you strike out with accuracy and a piercing bite.

CHALLENGES: Snakes have a certain impulse to hide and detach. When your work doesn't engage you, you retreat to your own inner world.

If you're good at slipping under the radar, it's possible nobody will even notice you falling behind. In this state you may begin to feel everything is meaningless.

To stave this off, pursue your passions! The arts can be a good way for you to express the things that only you seem to see. Only you get to decide what is meaningful to you. Chase it, and you may start to see how the rest of the world is connected. Even your most exasperating class has a role to play in the bigger picture.

ACTIVITIES WITH SNAKE SIGN ENERGY

- ◆ Psychology
- ◆ Acting
- ◆ Modern art
- ◆ Medicine

The Snake and Dragon are two sides of one coin. Where the Dragon excels by being filled to the brim, by being everything at once, the Snake excels through openness, through emptiness. A Snake sign is a blank canvas—they can become anything they want. Like the Dragon, the Snake also has a mystic quality, and is often drawn to the arts and the spiritual as ways to express their unique vision.

FINDING YOUR CENTER

Snakes are calm and introspective by nature. They don't often cling to the material world, preferring to turn their unblinking vision inward. However, this isn't always a relief. Snakes often struggle to find their center.

This is because Snakes often sense the truth: there is no true center because everything is moving all the time. The idea that we are the same from day to day is only that—an idea. It may be an idea held by many, but it's still just an idea. For you, freedom lies not in grasping at center but in letting go. Let yourself off the hook. Even just for a moment, give up the idea that there's something you *have* to succeed at, something you have to be, or something you must know. Let yourself live with no expectations for a minute, an hour, an afternoon. You might be surprised at what can emerge.

SNAKES IN CHINESE MYTH

The snake has long been seen as a mystic creature—its sinuous motion mysterious and magical, its shed skins and venom fangs implying a strange power over life and death. As such, its features appear in many Chinese deities such as Nüwa and Gonggong.

Said to be the creator of humankind, shaping us from riverside clay, Nüwa was a woman from the waist up and a snake from the waist down. Gonggong also had a snake's body and a man's head. An ancient water god, Gonggong lost a duel against the god of fire, and in his frustration smashed the Earth hard enough to tilt it. This caused horrible floods and disasters before Nüwa intervened to repair the damage. Nonetheless, some say the Earth remains a little tilted to this day.

A folktale also speaks of another famous snake. The beautiful Lady White Snake was a magical serpent who could take human form. She fell in love with a human man, and their epic romance had to overcome impossible odds: magical foes, their star-crossed backgrounds, and even death itself.

HOW TO SECURE GOOD LUCK

Like the elegant coral snake, the lucky colors of the Snake sign are black, red, and yellow. These colors emphasize the Snake's sense of style when you are in the mood to draw attention, but there's nothing wrong with keeping these colors close and secret as well. Your lucky numbers are 2, 8, and 9, so keep a lookout for any appearance of those numbers in any combination.

Orchids and cacti of all kinds are your lucky flowers, bringing good fortune and beauty alike.

THE YEAR OF THE SNAKE

Dragon and Snake are in many ways opposite, and the transition between the two Zodiac years might seem abrupt. Both represent potential, but while the Dragon's potential is active and bustling, the Snake's potential lies in openness and introspection.

After the high-flying Dragon, the year of the Snake is a time for looking inward for everyone, not just those with Snake in their birth chart. What have we accomplished? What do we hope for? Snake years are a time for beginnings, as we shrug off old forms and skins and enter what is mysterious and new with an open mind.

Beware that the sudden shift in pace can also make Snake years a time of low energy. We may think our pasts seem ridiculous, while the future seems a frightening mystery. Cut yourself some slack—you don't need all the answers right now. You can find meaning in your day in little things, five minutes at a time.

THE HORSE

YEAR: 1954, 1966, 1978, 1990, 2002, 2014, 2026, 2038
MONTH: June 6–July 7
HOUR: 11:00 a.m.–1:00 p.m.

Explosive and bold, the Horse rides in the heart of Summer and in the hours that surround high noon. If you were born during either of these times, the Horse is one of your signs! Full of passion and strength, the Horse is optimistic, independent, and often in motion.

FAMILY

The Horse loves to travel in herds, happy to have companions to race and show off for. Being around others pushes you to be your best. That said, the Horse also has an independent streak and will kick and buck before they break.

HOW TO EXPRESS LOVE: Unlike the Snake, the Horse is no mystery. Horses express feelings and affection plainly. For you, love is best expressed through shared activity. Find the activities that you and your loved ones both adore and make space in your life to participate in them together. Shared passion holds a simple and binding joy.

HOW TO BE HEARD: Horses are defined by a forceful strength, and this is as true in their conversations as it is in their actions. You may find you express yourself best when you just say what you feel, without over-thinking. But don't let expression stand in the way of listening—just because you have great ideas doesn't mean you're always right. Holding space for correction will give you flexibility and room for growth.

FRIENDSHIP

The sign of the Horse is a thrilling friend. People are drawn to your high energy and honest way of speaking, but you're happiest when surrounded by people who can push you and share the activities you love. The Tiger and Dog can meet your energy, while the nurturing Goat balances you.

BEING SUPPORTIVE: People are energized by your upbeat and honest company. But some may struggle to keep up with your hearty gallop. While it's great that you can lose yourself in your favorite activities, don't forget to check in with the people around you. If you see some-one lagging behind, perhaps you can give them a tip that will get them back into the action or make them feel valued as a part of the group. Remember, there are more ways to enjoy something than just being good at it. Sometimes it's enough to enjoy something for its own sake.

WORKING THROUGH PROBLEMS: You love to win an argument, but if a friend isn't seeing things your way after a couple of minutes, pushing them harder is unlikely to change their mind. People respond to the energy they're fed, and if you dig in your heels, your friends might do the same.

If an issue is too crucial to simply agree to disagree, try to courteously explain what is unacceptable to you and why. See if you can encourage the other person to do the same. Make them feel safe to open up. Are you both certain there's no room for compromise?

SCHOOL

STRENGTHS: Like the Ox, the Horse is associated with sheer power and ability to get things done. However, while the Ox works steadily, the Horse gets things done in brilliant bursts.

Play to your strengths by looking at school as a challenge, a chance to compete against yourself. Hands-on practice is where you excel, so participating often and putting yourself in the thick of things will help you learn. If light competition with your classmates pushes you to excel, this can work in your favor as well—though the best rivalries are built on mutual respect.

CHALLENGES: When the Horse is understimulated, its wild energy may result in distraction and troublemaking. Here are a couple strategies for refocusing:

- ◆ Set a timer for just ten minutes and see if you can keep yourself working for that long. When you finish, take a quick stretch or start another ten minutes if you're on a roll.

- ◆ Try to focus on just one task at a time. Get it done before moving on to the next.
- ◆ When you have a thought, instead of acting on it, try writing it down. Once it's written down you can always come back to it later if it still feels important.

ACTIVITIES WITH HORSE SIGN ENERGY

- ◆ Competitive sports (track, boxing, etc.)
- ◆ Playing outside
- ◆ Woodworking
- ◆ Landscaping/yard work

Any test of skill, especially in front of a crowd, carries the Horse sign's energy. The Horse sign thrives in the outdoors, competitive environments, and anything that involves physical space.

FINDING YOUR CENTER

You often find your center "in the zone": the swing of a bat, the stroke of a pen, the thrill of the moment. It's when your mind stops overthinking and everything just runs on autopilot. You can pursue this feeling by giving yourself the opportunity to do what you love, for no reason other than enjoying it.

That said, even the wildest Horse must occasionally rest. The Horse's unbridled bursts of energy can burn you out if you don't take care of yourself. If you feel tired, listless, or cranky, take a moment to check in. Is what you're doing right now necessary? Are you enjoying it? Would you be happier if you took a break? Make sure you're doing something because you want to, not just because it's there.

HORSES IN CHINESE MYTH

The Horse appears in Chinese folklore and myth often as a symbol of power and military strength.

Romance of the Three Kingdoms is an epic story, mythologizing a time when China was divided into three powerful kingdoms that warred for a hundred years. In wartime, great horses were as important as great soldiers. Red Hare was known as the swiftest and fiercest of all horses. With a coat of red and speed enough to travel a thousand miles in a single day, Red Hare would only permit the very strongest warriors to ride him, preferring to starve rather than carry a lesser fighter.

Another famous horse from a Chinese classic is the White Dragon Horse, ridden by the holy monk Tang Sanzang in the sixteenth-century novel *Journey to the West*. Originally a dragon prince who was sentenced to death for destroying a sacred pearl, he was offered an alternative penance: to take the form of a horse and bear the holy monk on his quest to retrieve Buddhist scriptures. Fighting and traveling alongside such famous figures as the Monkey King, White Dragon Horse was eventually granted a position in Heaven for his noble service.

HOW TO SECURE GOOD LUCK

The Horse's lucky colors are green, yellow, red, and purple, and 2, 3, and 7 are often considered their luckiest numbers. You don't need to change your life to make way for these numbers or colors, but keep an eye out! Seeing them might indicate something important is coming your way, and keeping them close will bring out the Horse's strength and independent spirit.

Your lucky flowers are jasmine and the calla lily.

THE YEAR OF THE HORSE

The time for action returns after the thoughtful introspection of the Snake, and this is the Horse's time to shine. Snake to Horse is a big transition, like invisible heat blossoming into brilliant flame.

Horse years are years for action, getting work done, and achievement for its own sake. This applies to everyone, not just those with Horse in their birth chart. Work often becomes most difficult when we overthink it, when we worry and allow it to loom over us, creating stress. The Horse teaches us an important lesson: sometimes your worries can become an obstacle. You know what to do, so just let yourself do it.

However, while Horse years can be times of galloping progress, the flip side of carefree is careless. It's too easy to trample things in the thrill of the race. Horse years can also be a time of restlessness if you don't have a good project to pour your energy into. A Horse must run, and without purpose it may run in the wrong direction.

THE GOAT

YEAR: 1955, 1967, 1979, 1991, 2003, 2015, 2027, 2039
MONTH: July 7–August 7
HOUR: 1:00 p.m.–3:00 p.m.

Nurturing and communal, the Goat defends the end of Summer and the early afternoon from one to three p.m. If you were born during either of these times, the Goat is one of your signs. Goat energy is interested in people and always attuned to their needs, often putting others ahead of the self.

FAMILY

On the farm and in the wild, Goats are herd animals, happiest when surrounded. Perhaps the most family-oriented sign in the entire Zodiac, the Goat embodies family's ideals of selflessness and unconditional love.

HOW TO EXPRESS LOVE: Goats show warmth by attending to loved ones, perhaps even making personal sacrifices to do so. While it's great to be there for others, it's important that you allow them to be there for you as well. This kind of mutual attention is what allows people to grow closer together. Your efforts toward care are futile if they're one-sided.

HOW TO BE HEARD: Goats sometimes struggle to express opinions that may cause conflict. Goats desire unity with their loved ones and at times may seem to merge into the people around them, becoming like an extension of others instead of their own person.

Expressing your opinions and thoughts, even if others think differently, isn't an obstacle to true togetherness, but rather a path toward it. Unless you are true to your feelings and express them, how can the people around you know the real you? Take heart—it is better to be messy and seen than inoffensive and invisible.

FRIENDSHIP

The Goat's sense of community isn't just about family. To the Goat, anybody can be family. On farms, the goat will bond with all kinds of animals: sheep, horses, people, even chickens.

BEING SUPPORTIVE: Goats derive their compassion from an understanding that all things are connected. Just as nature connects animals, plants, stones, and weather, we are connected to the people around us, even if we'd rather not be. Seeing how we are all one, the Goat is willing to self-sacrifice in the name of the community.

While there is nobility in this action, be aware of when you are doing this because you want to, and when you do it because you feel you have to. The former is noble, while the latter is a dangerous recipe for bitterness and resentment, eventually turning the Goat intolerant and ready to butt heads.

WORKING THROUGH PROBLEMS: Goats struggle with conflict, especially with friends. They are so interested in unity, it can be difficult for them to understand when people want different things or are fine leaving their differences unresolved. At their most vulnerable, Goats may become more like sheep, submitting to a herd mentality, rather than standing up for themselves.

Remember that sometimes the best way to serve others is by guiding them, and in order to guide, you must occasionally take the lead. Also be sure to respect the boundaries of the people around you. Some people may want more space than you do, and that's okay.

SCHOOL

STRENGTHS: Sweet, artistic, and receptive, Goats are well suited to the little communities formed by classrooms. They get along well with others, are team players, and have no problem following instructions. They like to form strong friend groups and relationships, and this can help them excel outside of class.

Play to your strengths by finding your crowd, the people you get along with and like to be around. Reach out to them when you need help, and you'll find you're stronger as a team than you are alone.

CHALLENGES: Goats can struggle under high-pressure environments. They are conflict averse, and if they think they may disappoint themselves or those around them, they may refuse to even try. They can end up going to surprising lengths to hide or avoid failure, even getting wrapped up in complicated lies. Try to avoid viewing life as something that can be won or lost. All that matters is the experience, and learning a little on the way.

ACTIVITIES WITH GOAT SIGN ENERGY

- ◆ Chorus
- ◆ Volunteering
- ◆ Dance
- ◆ Rock climbing

Activities that provide a sense of community or offer a creative outlet make natural hobbies for the Goat.

FINDING YOUR CENTER

Like many of the more sensitive signs, the Goat may sometimes feel overwhelmed. You are connected to so much of the world, and this can feel chaotic. When you are overwhelmed, take some time to unplug. Do something just for yourself, like taking a long walk, a hot bath, or reading a good book. The world is more durable than you think—you don't always need to think of ways to make it better. Rest, get away from it all, and take time to look inward instead. The world will still be there when you return.

GOATS IN CHINESE MYTH

You may have seen this sign referred to as the Sheep or Ram in other places. This is because ancient China didn't distinguish between goats and sheep and other caprine creatures—after all, they're closely related!

One famous myth involving goats is the story of the Five Immortals and the city of Guangzhou. It is said that in the ancient days of the city's founding a terrible drought choked the region. People suffered and starved until one day a strange music rose from the South China Sea. After this music came a five-colored cloud. Out of this cloud emerged Five Immortals, each wearing a different elemental color and riding a matching goat. Each Immortal carried a sheaf of rice they gave to the people. When it was planted, the rice sprouted up, plentiful and rich. The Immortals then rose away on the clouds, leaving their goats behind to watch over the city forever. This is the Goat's symbolic role—ever giving and self-sacrificing.

For this reason, Guangzhou is nicknamed the City of Five Goats to this day. If you visit, you can see statues of the goats carved in their honor in Yuexiu Park, or the Temple of Five Immortals, where the Immortals were once worshipped and honored.

HOW TO SECURE GOOD LUCK

The Goat's lucky colors are green, red, and purple, and its lucky numbers are 2 and 7. Combinations of these colors and numbers might suggest opportunity, or something you can rely on in a pinch.

Carnations and primrose bring you luck and can brighten your day with their joyful colors.

THE YEAR OF THE GOAT

As always, each year gives birth to its opposite. After the rushing and forceful Horse comes the delicate and harmonious Goat. One builds the backbone, the other forms beauty. Like stem and flower, both are necessary.

Goat years are generally peaceful. This applies to everyone, not just those who have a Goat in their birth chart. The Goat's values of community, service, and relationships rise to the top, and Goat years are often years of social awareness. We reevaluate our place in the world, rediscover the importance of our relationships, and ask questions about how to make the world a better, more equitable place. The Goat is a reformer, but unlike the rebellious Tiger, the Goat believes that understanding and reform from within are more effective tools for change than rebellion and uprising.

In the year of the Goat, beware of losing yourself in relationships or becoming overly dependent on the people around you to define you. Try to maintain a healthy independence—sacrificing yourself on the altar of others is unlikely to do good in the long run.

THE MONKEY

YEAR: 1956, 1968, 1980, 1992, 2004, 2016, 2028, 2040
MONTH: August 7–September 8
HOUR: 3:00 p.m.–5:00 p.m.

Intelligent and playful, the Monkey is the patron of those born in the start of Autumn and the hours of three to five p.m. If you were born during either of these times, the Monkey is one of your signs! Monkey signs see the world as one big puzzle, one big game to be solved and won. They enjoy being challenged and putting their intellect to the test.

FAMILY

Naturally social, most monkeys travel in troops. Monkey signs know there's no better intellectual challenge than figuring out other people.

HOW TO EXPRESS LOVE: Monkeys enjoy debate and discussion. Anyone who will join you in musing upon the secret workings of the world will have your affection. This can be a great bonding activity.

Monkeys enjoy games and can often locate the challenge in anything. Help your loved ones find the fun in any situation. Whether you're making lemonade out of lemons or being the life of the party, you will brighten everyone's day.

HOW TO BE HEARD: Monkeys are proud of their clever solutions and quick to notice the logical failings of others. When pointing out the holes in another person's story, be careful that you aren't hurting their feelings or invalidating their beliefs. Some people will see criticism as an attack even if you mean it to be constructive or in jest. You can still give people advice, but try to meet them where they are instead of where you are. Your wisdom will reach further if you prepare the other person to receive it.

FRIENDSHIP

Monkeys are impulsive and make fun wherever they go. Together with the Rat and Dragon, you are a team capable of solving any puzzle. The Rooster shares your eye for detail while the Snake shares your thoughtful and piercing view of the world.

BEING SUPPORTIVE: People are easily charmed by Monkeys—their playful antics, quick wit, and piercing insight. But Monkeys are selective about who they befriend. They like to seek out new experiences and new people, and they relish the idea that their friends are special. Don't be too quick to write people off just because they don't think the same way you do. Not everybody will be as quick as you, but if you let them get there, they may come up with ideas you never would have found on your own. There's more than one way to peel a banana.

WORKING THROUGH PROBLEMS: Monkeys are drawn to complicated problems, so they lean toward overcomplicated solutions. You are capable of composing intricate fantasies of what might or might not be, and you can get lost in your own games if you aren't careful. It is good for you to check in with the people around you so you know your vision of a problem aligns with reality. Don't try to solve everything on your own— some problems need to be worked on from both ends. You can't have a friendship alone, and you can't solve friendship problems alone either.

SCHOOL

STRENGTHS: Perhaps the sign most associated with intellect, Monkeys make natural scholars. Your curiosity about the world around you, combined with a head for puzzles, makes a natural fit for learning. Think of school as an opportunity to understand your world better, and use it as a tool to push open doors and broaden your horizons.

CHALLENGES: When insufficiently challenged, Monkey signs make their own challenges, and some might call this looking for trouble. Ask yourself, what aspects of class *do* interest you? What is interesting about them, and how can you chase that curiosity? Some areas of school give you freer rein, like extracurriculars and take-home projects. Use these opportunities to take control and explore the subjects *you* find interesting.

ACTIVITIES WITH MONKEY SIGN ENERGY

- ◆ Coding
- ◆ Improv
- ◆ Gaming
- ◆ Philosophy

Monkey energy thrives in anything that allows you to puzzle out difficult problems, engage in creative conversation, and find the fun hidden inside ordinary situations.

FINDING YOUR CENTER

Solving problems is one of the human brain's most fundamental desires, and this is where Monkey finds joy. After all, what are games and entertainment but problems and patterns for your brain to engage with? Whether your puzzle of choice is a video game or a math problem, anything that fully engages your brain will keep you entertained and relaxed.

On the other end of the spectrum, consider trying something that lets you turn *off* your brain for a change. Take a hot bath or do something that requires using your body more than your brain. There are times when the body knows what to do, how to move, and how to feel without the conscious mind being involved at all. Explore that zone, and you may find a new kind of peace entirely.

MONKEYS IN CHINESE MYTH

It would be impossible to talk about monkey myths without mentioning Sun Wukong. Also called the Monkey King, Sun Wukong is the hero of *Journey to the West*, a classic sixteenth-century novel.

Born from a magic stone, Sun Wukong was a monkey with incredible powers. Lifting mountains and circling the Earth in a single bound were easy for him, but Wukong also had an ingenious mind, full of curiosity and mischief. A prodigy, he quickly mastered a range of martial and mystic arts, becoming an invincible fighter with a host of magic powers, like shapeshifting, immortality, and duplication.

A Monkey sign's nature is to push and prod at the universe, to test and ask questions, and Sun Wukong embodied these qualities. Wukong's pursuit of respect led him to fight with the forces of Heaven and Hell alike, defeating every celestial army, warrior, and trap until finally the Buddha sealed him under a magic mountain. Here Wukong remained until he could put his skills to good use. After the holy monk Tang Sanzang freed him, the Monkey King joined a team of immortals and demons on their quest for Buddhist scriptures. Learning much from this shared journey, the Monkey King ultimately ascended to enlightenment, becoming the Buddha of Victorious Battle.

From irrepressible trickster to enlightened sage, the Monkey sign is energized by a balance of mischief and wisdom.

HOW TO SECURE GOOD LUCK

The Monkey's lucky colors are white, gold, and blue. Clothes, accessories, and charms in these colors may bring you the Monkey's playfulness and piercing wisdom. Look out for the numbers 1, 7, and 8. For the Monkey these numbers imply opportunity, significance, or a challenge yet to be explored, especially when they appear together.

The Monkey's lucky flower is the chrysanthemum, whose elegant petals hint at the puzzles and patterns hidden in plain sight.

THE YEAR OF THE MONKEY

After the Goat year reminds us of our role as part of a flock, the Monkey arrives to innovate and challenge. Like the Tiger, the Monkey's opposite on the Zodiac wheel, the Monkey inspires change. But where the Tiger's revolution is driven by passion and strength, the Monkey's is driven by intellect and curiosity.

The year of the Monkey is a time for discovery, innovation, and play. This applies to everyone, not just those with Monkey in their birth chart. It is a time for us to confront the things we believe in, and the ways those ideas might be foolish. It is the Monkey's way to point out our absurdities.

In a Monkey year, be cautious of narratives, the stories you tell yourself about yourself. Monkeys are the animal closest to humans, and they share many of our weaknesses. We are wickedly smart, but we are also capable of deluding ourselves. We tell ourselves comfortable lies and forget the difference between what we believe and what is true.

THE ROOSTER

YEAR: 1957, 1969, 1981, 1993, 2005, 2017, 2029, 2041
MONTH: September 8–October 8
HOUR: 5:00 p.m.–7:00 p.m.

Eloquent, elegant, and controlling, the Rooster watches the middle of Autumn as the leaves turn orange and gold. They also command the hours of five to seven p.m., when chickens traditionally come home to roost. If you're born during either of these times, the Rooster is one of your signs.

FAMILY

Rulers of the roost, Roosters are natural protectors of social order. You are aware of the people around you and unafraid to crow out to prevent disaster. You are most pleased when everything is just so, and appreciate when your hard work is properly recognized.

HOW TO EXPRESS LOVE: Roosters like to have projects. Joint commitments where you organize or make something together can bring you and your loved ones closer together. Just try to remember that togetherness and having a good time are more important than perfection.

Arts and crafts can also be a good way for you to make the most of your strengths. With an artist's eye and a strong sense of focus, you can make beautiful gifts that demonstrate your attention and care.

HOW TO BE HEARD: Roosters are known for their crow. They are highly social animals who vocalize all day long, organizing the chickens around them and warning off danger or misbehavior. Vocal and keen-eyed, you speak your mind decisively when you let yourself. You have a critical eye and may be eager to offer your critiques. It's great to be able to say what you believe, but remember to keep an open mind to other points of view as well. Roosters are good at convincing themselves that their way is the only way.

FRIENDSHIP

Confident, outgoing, and stylish, Roosters love an audience that can appreciate their wit and skill. The Ox and Snake make natural companions, both reliable and supportive. The Monkey shares your quick wit and love of challenge, while the Dragon shares your imperial sense of confidence and style.

BEING SUPPORTIVE: Roosters want to be liked and work very hard to be likable. From the way you dress to the way you act, you are often trying to put your best foot forward. When it comes to making new friends, this can work well. People appreciate your effort.

However, it's okay to let down your hair with the close friends you trust. Allowing yourself to be imperfect, asking for help, or admitting when you've made a mistake can be powerful ways to show trust. Once you get used to it, you may even find it's a relief to not always have to be flawless, and your friends will feel closer to the real you as a result.

WORKING THROUGH PROBLEMS: Roosters are quick to notice when something is going wrong, and eager to speak their minds. Direct communication is a great superpower as long as you address the problems with kindness and remain open to other viewpoints.

That said, not every problem has a solution, or even needs to be solved. When someone opens up to you about their troubles, it's okay to take a moment to clarify what this person needs. Are they seeking advice? Or do they just want support? Sometimes all we need is a shoulder to lean on.

SCHOOL

STRENGTHS: An eye for detail is an asset in most classrooms, and you succeed at any subject that you put your full attention to. Checklists, calendars, and plans of action all harness your sign's energy well. Being unafraid to speak up in class is a good way to push yourself and stay engaged. With some practice, you can excel at making your points clearly and compellingly, a skill that will serve you your whole life.

CHALLENGES: A sharp eye can lead to perfectionism, which can lead to constant criticism of yourself and others. But total control is an illusion anyway. Things will go wrong and mistakes will be made no matter what.

It is not your job to stop every mistake or mete out punishment. Move forward. Each mistake is just a stepping stone to progress.

ACTIVITIES WITH ROOSTER SIGN ENERGY

◆ Directing

◆ Crafts

◆ Gymnastics

◆ Ballroom dance

Anything that requires fine and delicate control, from art to engineering to leadership, is the Rooster through and through. Roosters are both skillful workers and decisive leaders, as both skills require the same deft hand.

FINDING YOUR CENTER

When agitated and overworked, Roosters may pick other people and themselves apart in their pursuit of exactness. To relax, try letting yourself off the hook. Not everything needs to be perfect, and it certainly doesn't need to be perfect *right now*. When you feel like you're going in circles, step away and come back when you feel better. Get out of your head and back into your body, whether that's by taking a shower, eating a hot meal, or going on a brisk walk where you take time to notice your surroundings. Consider having a relaxing day just for yourself, with no important projects or expectations. Even a Rooster has to rest its wings sometimes.

ROOSTERS IN CHINESE MYTH

As the only bird in the Zodiac, the Rooster sign is also used to represent other birds—the crane, owl, crow, and mythical birds as well.

The Sanzuwu is one such bird, also known as the three-legged crow who carries the sun. Originally, there were ten of the Sanzuwu, each with its own sun. They took turns flying across the sky, bringing light and warmth to the Earth. One day they all took flight together, and ten suns scorched a wasted streak across the Earth. The archer Houyi was summoned, and he shot down all the birds but one. There remains one sun and one Sanzuwu to this day.

Another bird associated with the Rooster sign is the Fenghuang. Also called the Chinese Phoenix, it had feathers in each of the five fundamental colors of ancient China: red, yellow, azure, black, and white. The Fenghuang was considered the symbol of the Empress the same way the Imperial Dragon was the symbol of the Emperor. While the Imperial Dragon represents the Earth and water at the center of our lives, the Fenghuang represents the skies that seem to spin around us: the planets and stars, the moon and sun.

Thanks to these birds, the Rooster sign itself is often linked to the rising sun. Who else crows to welcome it every morning?

HOW TO SECURE GOOD LUCK

Gold, yellow, and brown are the Rooster's lucky colors. Yellow is the color of the Emperor—it is the color of the Earth as well as the center of the compass rose. Your lucky numbers are 5, 7, and 8. When you see them, take a moment to look for hidden beauty in the world around you.

Your lucky flowers are the gladiolus, cockscomb, and impatiens.

THE YEAR OF THE ROOSTER

After the Monkey takes everything apart, the careful Rooster puts it back together. Rooster years are a time of analysis, planning, and control. This applies to everyone, not just those with Rooster in their birth chart. It's a time to see the problems and obstacles around us and make plans to overcome them.

While planning, look forward without becoming set on a single outcome. If you can plan for the future while remaining open to possibilities, you will be well positioned to spread your wings.

The year of the Rooster is an important time for self-care and relaxation. Otherwise, such constant vigilance may burn you out. You may also find that more conflicts arise in Rooster years, as more people notice their problems with one another and vocalize them. This energy doesn't have to be destructive. If you can remain open-minded and kind, it can be a tool for communication, allowing you and the people around you to resolve and let go of problems.

THE DOG

YEAR: 1958, 1970, 1982, 1994, 2006, 2018, 2030
MONTH: October 8–November 7
HOUR: 7:00 p.m.–9:00 p.m.

Diligent and loyal, the Dog guards the hours from seven to nine p.m. and the end of Autumn. If you were born during either of these times, the Dog is one of your signs! Both a guardian and a companion, you will do anything for your family, friends, or favorite cause. You may be wary around strangers, but once they earn your trust, you stand by them no matter what.

FAMILY

Dogs love to be part of a pack! When the Dog is included and cared for, nobody is happier and more loving. But when surrounded by strangers, they can become nervous and wary. If you feel your loved ones are treating you as an outsider, you may find yourself snapping back at them. Dogs are known for their devotion, but they're also known for their bark!

HOW TO EXPRESS LOVE: Showing love to people you trust comes naturally to the Dog. Wag your tail for someone else's passion, whether it's a sport, book, or quirky interest, and the good feeling will be contagious.

HOW TO BE HEARD: Obedient and trustworthy, some Dogs are more responsive to other people's needs than their own. Remember, there's no shame in letting your loved ones know when you're worried or uncomfortable. If you can communicate calmly and clearly, the people around you will only respect you more for helping them understand who you are.

FRIENDSHIP

The sign of the Dog is a fantastic friend. A loyal supporter and great source of comfort and nonjudgmental advice in times of trouble, they tend to mesh well with the Tiger, Horse, Pig, and Rabbit.

BEING SUPPORTIVE: For the Dog, the earliest stages of friendship feel the most difficult. It's hard to fight your instinct to growl at every stranger, and hard to know when they've earned your trust. Don't be afraid to make the first move around potential friends! Just taking an interest in other people's lives and passions will draw them to you. If you have a good time together, it will become that much easier to reach out again later. And if you don't click, that's fine too—make like a wet dog, shake it off, and move on.

Long-term friendships are often much easier for the Dog, after you've worked out the level of support and trust that each person is looking for. In good times and bad, nothing beats the comfort of a loyal canine friend.

WORKING THROUGH PROBLEMS: Despite their pack instinct, many Dogs have a streak of lone wolf in them, especially when feeling vulnerable. You might keep people away, even while deep down you want reassurance. Talking to your friends about your needs and boundaries can be a good way to make you feel safe, and can make you more comfortable demonstrating vulnerability in the future.

If your friends ever make you feel more defensive than loved, don't be afraid to branch out and seek friends in new places. Leaving a pack behind is hard for most Dogs, but it's much worse to stay with people who misuse your loyalty or kick you around. One rough patch doesn't mean you should give up on old friends, but it's okay to give a little space for people to come around. Keep an open heart and you will gravitate naturally to the people who make you feel safest.

SCHOOL

STRENGTHS: Eager, attentive, and obedient, Dog signs have great potential as students. You're at your best when you actually enjoy the assignment, but can find gratification in any task well done.

When it comes to group work, you can hold the pack together. You pull your weight, inspire others, and enjoy a bit of attention and competition. To capitalize on your strengths, give yourself clear goals to meet and try to work with others who are excited about the material. You may find their excitement rubs off on you!

CHALLENGES: You have a keen nose for when trouble's brewing, but sometimes it can be too sensitive for your own good. It's easy for you to imagine the disasters lurking around each corner and end up barking at every shadow. Overstimulated, you may work yourself into a frenzy. When it all feels like too much, start by tackling one problem at a time. If you can't get it all done, it's not the end of the world. Do what you can, and you may be surprised by how much you achieve.

ACTIVITIES WITH DOG SIGN ENERGY

- Going for walks
- Martial arts
- Debate
- Team sports (like basketball or soccer)

Teamwork, the outdoors, and competition are all things that bring out the Dog sign's attributes: exuberance and passionate pursuit of goals.

FINDING YOUR CENTER

The Dog works hard and plays hard, so make sure you take some time to let yourself rest. If it's nice out, going for a quiet walk with someone who makes you feel relaxed can be a nice middle ground. It will engage you physically and socially while also giving you a chance to reset and recharge.

A short Dog-nap can be even more rejuvenating, and luxurious as well. After a long, exciting day, there's nothing more rewarding than well-earned sleep. Good food and proper rest are the cradle of energy and allow you to make the most of each day.

DOGS IN CHINESE MYTH

Chinese myth includes many famous dogs! Panhu was a dragon dog who became human after defeating a mighty general no man was brave enough to challenge. For his heroic deed he was married to the Emperor's daughter, and their children went on to rule a powerful kingdom.

Another mighty dog of legend is the Tiangou, a dog who became huge and immortal after licking up a leftover immortality pill meant for his owners. Tiangou chases the sun and moon, causing an eclipse whenever he finally catches one in his mouth. To this day it is tradition to make noise and light firecrackers during an eclipse to warn Tiangou, "Bad dog, spit it out!" But who can blame a dog for wanting to chase a ball? When on good behavior, Tiangou faithfully guards the gates of Heaven and watches over weary travelers.

HOW TO SECURE GOOD LUCK

The Dog's lucky colors are generally considered to be red, green, and purple. Consider carrying a small significant object with these colors in a pocket, pouch, or backpack. Small mementos like dice, paper notes, or other keepsakes that mean something to you can remind you of all the good in your life and bring feelings of loyalty and connection. If the universe offers you something in green, purple, or red, it may be a sign of good fortune coming your way!

The Dog's lucky numbers are 3, 4, 9, and any combination of those digits. Their lucky flowers are the rose and the cymbidium orchid.

THE YEAR OF THE DOG

After the proud Rooster scouts the grounds and crows its orders, the cheerful Dog romps and obeys. Dog years are good for achievement and for shoring up what we already have. This applies to everyone, not just those with Dog in their birth chart. Boundaries are both tested and reinforced as the Dog protects its territory but also sniffs curiously at its edges. The year of the Dog is a good time for strengthening bonds as Dog years emphasize loyalty and bring us all closer together. Try to make time for people you love—whether that's working on a project, taking walks, enjoying a meal together, or just lazing around in the sun.

On the flip side, the Dog's anxious and suspicious side may come out in a Dog year too, so do your best to keep your doubts at arm's length. Remind yourself that while boundaries are good, walls that are too thick can become a cage. Do your best to bark less and wag more, and the Dog year will bring you all the exuberance and love of our favorite canine companions.

THE PIG

YEAR: 1959, 1971, 1983, 1995, 2007, 2019, 2031
MONTH: November 7–December 7
HOUR: 9:00 p.m.–11:00 p.m.

Honest and content, the Pig rests in the sleepy hours from nine to eleven p.m. and guides the beginning of Winter. People born during either of these times can look to the Pig as one of their signs! Pigs enjoy comfort and kindness. They live in the moment, and while they can appreciate any place or anyone, they have a special fondness for the people and places they call home.

FAMILY

Lovers of stability and comfort, Pig signs are peacemakers. Sweet-tempered and generous, your sincere appreciation for the people you love makes everyone feel more at home. In the old days, owning pigs was a sign of a family's wealth and stability, and you too can bring your home prosperity and joy.

HOW TO EXPRESS LOVE: Pigs have a knack for seeing good in people. Just as they pick sweet truffles out of the messiest dirt, Pigs can always find what's wonderful about the people around them. Tell others when you admire something about them. Showing people that their hard work, style, or other lovable qualities have not gone unappreciated will let them know you care.

HOW TO BE HEARD: On the other hand, Pigs are so naturally adaptable, sometimes they find it hard to recognize their own discomfort. If you're ever concerned about how things are going, it's okay to express your doubts to the people around you. When you talk through your worries, you'll understand them better, and also help make others aware of your concern.

FRIENDSHIP

Pigs are lovable and dependable friends. Diplomats who want nothing but happiness for themselves and the people around them, Pigs especially get along with the Rabbit, Goat, Dog, and Tiger.

BEING SUPPORTIVE: The Pig's warm and easygoing manner makes you easy to talk to. Pigs are islands of peace in a chaotic farm, and your friends appreciate your grounded reliability.

Pig signs may feel more comfortable following another person's lead in a friendship than setting their own pace. And that adaptability is very noble! But don't forget a friendship goes both ways. If you like being around somebody, it's okay to reach out to them first. This will help them feel wanted, and help you spend more time with the people you like.

WORKING THROUGH PROBLEMS: Sometimes Pigs have trouble sticking up for themselves. Don't let yourself get stuck in the mud. Supporting your friends is important but so is supporting yourself! When in doubt, it's okay to stop and ask yourself what *you* want, and make that preference known.

Though you may not always realize it, self-care is important to Pig signs. If you need to take time off to care for yourself, do it! Letting yourself wallow once in a while will leave you more clearheaded and refreshed in the long run. Taking a step back can also give you a chance to examine your feelings.

Pigs struggle with conflict and may find it easier to bury problems than address them. If there's something on your mind, consider writing it down in a journal or unsent letter first. This can help you organize your thoughts and find your voice when the time comes.

SCHOOL

STRENGTHS: Many people think of Pig signs as lucky, but really Pigs make their own luck. Your good nature makes life look simple, even when you're working very hard. You might procrastinate, but you have an ability to get work done with incredible speed and skill when you set your mind to it.

You are at your happiest when surrounded by familiar faces and routines, so the longer the school year goes on, the more things start to click for you. Play to this strength by taking steps to make school feel more like home. Build routines you feel comfortable with, and try to make at least one friend in each class you find yourself in.

CHALLENGES: Pigs like to do activities at their own pace, and if a project or subject doesn't interest them, they may go out of their way to avoid it. They also appreciate pleasure and fun, and can get easily caught up in addictive distractions. Setting schedules and designated workdays can help you move work from a "maybe tomorrow" to a "why not today?" state of mind. When you actually commit and get in the zone, you often find the time flies, so give yourself a chance to get there.

ACTIVITIES WITH PIG SIGN ENERGY

◆ Baking (and sharing)
◆ Band
◆ Tech crew
◆ Film club/movie night

Any activity where the Pig can find close friends and provide for them is one where the Pig will be happy.

FINDING YOUR CENTER

The Pig has a strong work ethic yet also enjoys relaxing and enjoying the moment. Sometimes this can lead to inner conflict. Your ability to relax and make the most of life is wonderful, but Pig signs feel most fulfilled when they can also make progress on a worthwhile project.

Pick a long-term project that makes you happy to work on. It could be a skill you've always wanted to practice, a book you've wanted to read, or a long-term achievement you've been meaning to finish. Start by trying to find just ten minutes each day to work on it, and you'll find yourself getting in the zone. Pigs require a lot of mental stimulation, and just a little bit of consistent productivity can free up your conscience when you call it a day.

PIGS IN CHINESE MYTH

The most famous pig in Chinese literature is Zhu Bajie. Part pig and part exiled god, Zhu Bajie joined Tang Sanzang and the Monkey King in their fabled journey west to retrieve Buddhist scrolls. Superstrong, shapeshifting, and able to ride on clouds, Zhu Bajie was one of the most powerful members of the team, famous for his incredible appetites and nine-toothed fighting rake.

Another pig from Chinese myth is the Bingfeng. A mysterious creature from a distant land across the sea, this black pig has two heads, one on its front and one on its back. Which is which, who can say? Some joke that this made it hard for the Bingfeng to make any decisions because for one head to go forward, the other had to go backward! But others see it as more of a blessing than a curse—the Bingfeng is two in one, a lifelong and unbreakable partnership.

HOW TO SECURE GOOD LUCK

The Pig is one of the signs most associated with luck! Yellow, gold, and brown are colors thought to bring out the Pig's luck and association with wealth. You don't need to go out of your way or change the way you dress, but keep in mind that a yellow flourish or a metal accessory like a bracelet or ring can help signal confidence and flare.

The Pig's lucky numbers are 2, 5, and 8, and any combinations of those digits. Their lucky flowers are the hydrangea and daisy.

THE YEAR OF THE PIG

After the Dog watches and protects, the Pig nestles down to enjoy that security. Pig years are good for relaxation and enjoyment. This applies to everyone, not just those with Pig in their birth chart. Eat, sleep, nourish yourself. Live in the moment, take things as they are, and don't overthink.

Pig years emphasize our relationship with relaxation and pleasure. If those things are difficult for you, a year of the Pig can be challenging. Try not to spread yourself too thin, and don't starve your mind and body of the stimulation they need. The time to start new things will come, but the Pig is the Zodiac that brings things full circle to the end, like a curly pig tail.

Honesty comes easily during Pig years, so slow down and take stock of what you've already achieved. Though you have reached the end of the Zodiac cycle, could it be that something is just beginning?

COMBINATIONS

———————◦⦿◦———————

NOW THAT WE KNOW THE ANIMALS, WE CAN TALK ABOUT THE ways they harmonize, conflict, and combine. Just like atoms can lock together to form new molecules, the twelve animals can combine to create new patterns entirely.

Combinations of animals can be formed with just a person's own horoscope, perhaps describing inner strengths or conflicts. They can also form *between* people—between yourself and a friend, for instance—suggesting ways that different people may or may not work together. Finally, combinations can also form between a person and a certain period of time—a certain hour, day, month, or year—suggesting the kind of fortune that time might bring.

In ancient days this knowledge was used often to make predictions about the future.

MATCHING PAIRS

These pairs can be found by drawing parallel lines across the Zodiac wheel, preceding from Rat/Ox, to Pig/Tiger, to Dog/Rabbit, all the way to Goat/Horse.

Generally considered a good omen, each of these pairs represents unlikely partners who bring balance to one another, and work well together. Each pairing also correlates to a specific element. Tiger/Pig creates Wood energy, Rat/Ox creates Earth energy, Dragon/Rooster creates Metal energy, Monkey/Snake creates Water energy, and Dog/ Rabbit and Horse/Goat both create Fire energy.

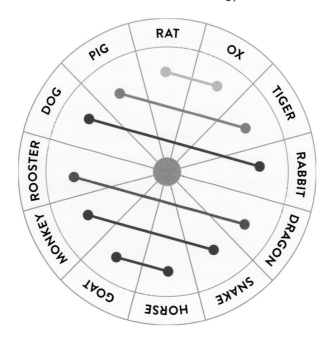

WITHIN: When such a pair occurs within a person's own Zodiac, it can suggest unique talents, or a kind of balance the person needs to strive for. Depending on the pair, it may also reveal a hidden Wǔxíng element.

WITH OTHERS: When these pairs occur between different people, it suggests they have potential together. Either they cover one another's weaknesses, see eye to eye, or can expand each other's horizons.

WITH TIME: When moments in time, such as the year, form a transform-ing pair with someone's Zodiac, it usually represents an opportunity for change. The appearance of an unexpected elemental energy is also something to pay attention to.

CONFLICTING PAIRS

These pairs can be found by drawing parallel lines across the Zodiac wheel perpendicular to the matching pairs. These precede from Rabbit/Dragon, to Tiger/Snake, to Ox/Horse, all the way to Rooster/Dog.

Generally considered a warning, these pairs represent the potential for conflict. Remember these pairs do *not* mean automatic doom or disaster. Really, these pairs are very useful in suggesting ways we can better ourselves, strengthen our relationships, and avoid problems before they arise.

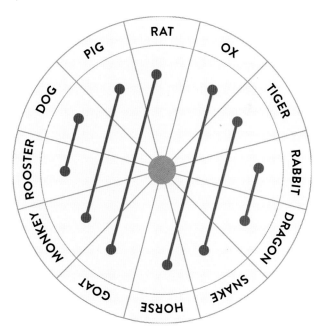

WITHIN: When such a pair occurs within a person's own Zodiac, it can suggest inner conflicts, competing desires, worries and anxieties, or conflicts with one's surroundings. Pay attention to the animals involved. What kind of conflict is being described? Is there a way to find balance, and bring out the best in both animals?

WITH OTHERS: When these pairs occur between different people, it suggests the potential for misunderstanding or conflict. Consider the animals involved. How do these animals tend to misunderstand one another? Does this describe a current conflict, or rather one to watch out for in the future?

WITH TIME: When moments in time, such as the year, form a conflicting pair with someone's Zodiac, it usually represents risk. Take a look at the interloping sign, and ask yourself what kind of risk that sign brings, and how you can prepare yourself to be ready for it.

OPPOSITES

Another kind of special pairing can be found by drawing lines directly through the center of the Zodiac wheel and connecting each

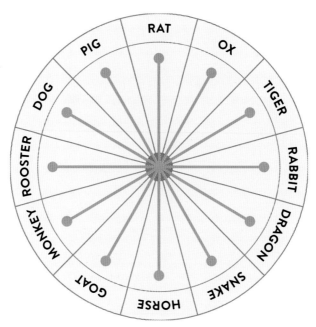

animal with its opposite. Rat/Horse, Ox/Goat, Tiger/Monkey, Rabbit/Rooster, etc.

Generally speaking, these combinations are about difference and suggest animals that are in some ways opposite to one another. The Horse is direct while the Rat is avoidant. The Snake is spiritual while the Pig is physical. The Tiger is an active body while the Monkey is an active mind.

Whether within or without, these pairings can be especially difficult to manage—as it is difficult to balance both sides of one coin. But they are also one of the most rewarding pairings to harmonize, as animals in opposition united provide the widest spectrum of wisdom and experience.

To achieve this harmony, remember that neither side of this pairing is correct or incorrect—they are both ways to experience the world, with each providing unique insight and joy.

COMPASS TRIOS

In addition to pairs, there are also significant trios of animals to keep in mind.

The most important are the Compass Trios. Each of these trios forms a triangle that points North, South, East, or West, and is associated with that direction, as well as with a specific element from the Wǔxíng. A full triangle is almost always lucky, suggesting great potential for a specific skill.

It is rare to find a whole triangle contained within a single person, but such good omens can often be sought out and created between two people, or between one person and a certain period of time.

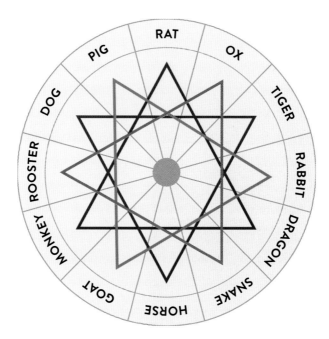

THE EAST TRIANGLE: Formed by the Rabbit, Goat, and Pig, this triangle is associated with Wood. United, this trio represents care, empathy, and an open mind. Together they have potential for healing and nurturing, made up of people who are diplomatic, artistic, and skilled at fostering happiness.

THE SOUTH TRIANGLE: Formed by the Horse, Tiger, and Dog, this triangle is associated with Fire. Also called the Hunting Trio, these signs are associated with action, excellence, victory, and competition. United, they indicate ambition, drive, and an unstoppable passion.

THE WEST TRIANGLE: Formed by the Rooster, Ox, and Snake, this triangle is associated with Metal. Together, this trio represents practicality. Cautious, hardworking, and calculating, this trio knows their goals and how to achieve them.

THE NORTH TRIANGLE: Formed by the Rat, Dragon, and Monkey, this triangle is associated with Water. United, this trio represents creativity, innovation, and intellect, a group that has not only great ideas but the resourcefulness and cunning to make them reality.

Notably there is no trio associated with the Earth! This is because the Earth is related not to a direction but rather to the center, around which all things revolve.

SEASONAL TRIOS

The Seasonal Trios are another set of trios made from the three animals whose months make up a full season, each a solid quadrant of the Zodiac wheel. While not as powerful as the Compass Trios, the Season Trios are useful for understanding how the animals relate to one another as parts of a never-ending cycle. Each season correlates to a Wǔxíng

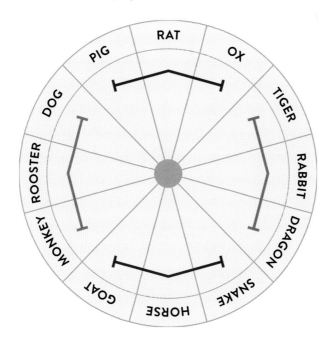

element. The trio of animals that make up that season thus manifests either Wood, Fire, Metal, or Water in abundance.

THE SPRING TRIO: Formed by the Tiger, Rabbit, and Dragon, this trio is associated with Wood. A complete Spring Trio likewise suggests an open and youthful heart.

THE SUMMER TRIO: Formed by the Snake, Horse, and Goat, this trio is associated with Fire. A complete Summer Trio thus indicates a passionate and bold spirit.

THE AUTUMN TRIO: Formed by the Monkey, Rooster, and Dog, this trio is associated with Metal. A complete Autumn Trio indicates a judicious and discerning mind.

THE WINTER TRIO: Formed by the Pig, Rat, and Ox, this trio is associated with Water. A complete Winter Trio suggests a profound and resilient soul.

Again, there is no Seasonal Trio associated with the Earth! Just as the Earth has no direction, it also has no season. Rather, it represents the transitions between the seasons, the places where seasons change, end, and begin again.

CROSSES

Finally, between the twelve animals there are also three key groups of four, each of which forms a perfect "cross," or square, within the Zodiac wheel. Composed of two complementary sets of opposites, a cross—whether it's within oneself, between people, or between a person and a certain period of time—is always an extreme result, and quite rare, and considered to be very powerful.

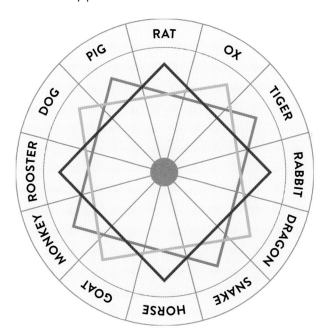

THE PEACH BLOSSOM: Formed by the Rat, Rabbit, Horse, and Rooster (one animal from each point of the compass), the Peach Blossom is about social skills, and the ability to influence anyone from any corner of the Earth. The Peach Blossom is the center. If you find yourself in this cross, be confident and listen kindly, not to impress others but for your own sake. Do this, and you will naturally draw success and love toward you.

THE EARLY SEASONS: Formed by the Tiger, Snake, Monkey, and Pig (the animals that represent the first months of each season), the Early Seasons cross represents growth, activity, and travel. Often it suggests a journey. If you find yourself in this cross, don't be afraid to try new things, explore, and come home wiser. Distance can be more about feeling than about miles. A journey can occur in your own backyard. Seek new experiences, and the world will unfold for you.

THE FOUR EARTHS: Formed by the Ox, Dragon, Goat, and Dog (animals associated with the Wǔxíng element of Earth), the Four Earths cross suggests both stability and complexity. If you find yourself in this configuration, know that anything is possible so long as you commit. Bring diligence and patience, and in time you can master anything.

CONCLUSION

THIS IS THE END—OR IS IT?

If you're interested in learning more about the Bāzi and Chinese astrology, this book is only the tip of the iceberg! Chinese astrology goes back thousands of years, with branches as thick and long as the oldest tree. There's always more out there for a curious soul.

Lastly, a reminder: the point of the Chinese Zodiac isn't to tell you who you are, or who you should be.

"Who am I?" is a question we never stop asking. Like all the oldest questions, it has no correct answer. The point is to ask, to reevaluate, and to discover. This is how we grow.

The Chinese Zodiac is one more way to explore this question and all the others nested inside it: How can I be a good family member? A good friend? How should I chase my dreams? Which dreams should I chase?

It's too easy to barrel forward in life without ever asking why. But by wrestling with important questions, we gain the power we need to steer our lives. By learning where we've come from, where we are, and where we still want to go, we can be active participants in life, building the roads we want to travel.

Your Zodiac is meant to speak to these possible roads, the people you might be and the things you might try. The answers will not all come right away, but I hope this book leaves you with questions.

How you answer is up to you.

RESOURCES

Aijmer, Göran. *New Year Celebrations in Central China in Late Imperial Times*. Hong Kong: The Chinese University of Hong Kong Press, 2003.

Done, Gregory David. "The 12 Characters of Destiny." Tiger's Play Astrology. Accessed November 11, 2021. www.tigersplayastrology.com/tigers-play/category/12-animals.

"Hsia Calendar (Ten Thousand Year Calendar)." n.d. Accessed January 9, 2022. www.hsiacalendar.com/.

Lai, T. C. *Animals of the Chinese Zodiac*. Hong Kong: Hong Kong Book Centre, 1979.

S.T., Althea. *A Course in Chinese Astrology: Reveal Your Destiny, Harness Your Luck with Four Pillars*. CreateSpace Publishing, 2017.

Walters, Derek. *The Chinese Astrology Workbook: How to Calculate and Interpret Chinese Horoscopes*. Northamptonshire: The Aquarian Press, 1988.

Walters, Derek. *The Secrets of Chinese Astrology*. Great Britain: Octopus Publishing, 2003.

Wen, Benebell. *The Tao of Craft: Fu Talismans and Casting Sigils in the Eastern Esoteric Tradition*. Berkeley, California: North Atlantic Books, 2016.

White, Suzanne. *The New Chinese Astrology*. New York: St. Martin's Press, 1993.

Wu, Shelly. *The Definitive Book of Chinese Astrology*. Red Wheel/Weiser, 2010.

Wu, Zhongxian. *The 12 Chinese Animals: Create Harmony in your Daily Life through Ancient Chinese Wisdom*. London: Singing Dragon, 2010.

Yap, Joey. *BaZi – The Destiny Code*. JY Books Sdn Bhd, 2005.

Yoke, Ho Peng. *Chinese Mathematical Astrology*. New York: Routledge, 2004.

Your Chinese Astrology. "Chinese Calendar, Tung Shing." Accessed November 11, 2021. www.yourchineseastrology.com/calendar/.

ACKNOWLEDGMENTS

THIS BOOK COULD NEVER HAVE BEEN BORN WITHOUT THE knowledge and skill of so many people.

Thank you to Ada Zhang for introducing me to this world and showing me how it's done. Having you look over a draft and fix so many of my concerns in a single go was always the greatest relief. Thanks to Cisca Schreefel for your hard work and attention to the little things. To Ana Maria-Bonner, the world of publicity is strange and fascinating, and so thank you for holding my hand through my first ever Instagram posts.

Thanks to everybody who let me read their horoscope in pursuit of my own understanding. You know who you are, and I hope that my readings brought you joy and fortune alike.

Also, to my dear friends, family, and teachers: I could never have come so far without you.

And last but not least, thanks to Qu Lan for the wonderful art that brings this book to life. It's magic, and I think the world deserves that.

ABOUT THE AUTHOR
AND ILLUSTRATOR

AARON HWANG is a writer with a passion for magic and learning about the way things work. He enjoys podcasts, board games, and all things nerdy. He is sometimes spotted looking pensively off into the distance, but he is not in thought; he is actually just spacing out. A graduate of Yale and the Iowa Writer's Workshop, Aaron is also the author of *The Chinese Zodiac: And Other Paths to Luck, Riches & Prosperity* for adults.

QU LAN was born and raised in China. After graduating in oil painting from the China Academy of Art, she moved to France and worked as a graphic designer in agencies. She then discovered the passion for illustration and launched her career as a freelance illustrator. Now she collaborates with numerous major publishers and companies. Her artwork is exhibited regularly and has received awards around the world.